ZEN AND THE ART OF GENTLE RETIREMENT

Zen and The Art of Gentle Retirement

Harry Turner

JANUS PUBLISHING COMPANY
London, England

First published in Great Britain 2009
by Janus Publishing Company Ltd,
105–107 Gloucester Place,
London W1U 6BY

www.januspublishing.co.uk

British Library Cataloguing-in-Publication Data
A catalogue record for this book is available from the British Library

ISBN 978-1-85756-760-1

Cover Design: Edwin Page

Printed and bound in Great Britain

Dedication

For my wife Carolyn,
to whom I have been married for 53 years,

Contents

Contents

Contents

Contents

Prologue

The word 'retirement' when coupled with those two chilling adjectives 'old' and 'age' can conjure up conflicting visions in the minds of those of an imaginative disposition. Some of these images are benign, others frankly apocalyptic.

So whether you are a gibbering, pessimistic ninny or a sunny, well-grounded optimist, this book can help you. Let's deal with the less palatable images of old age and retirement first, provided you are sitting comfortably.

A cursory glance at *Roget's Thesaurus* gives us a chilling take on old age and ageing. Here's just a few of things Roget associates with the ageing process. See if you don't immediately observe the umbilical connection with old-age pensioners themselves.

- Deterioration
- Declining
- Dilapidated
- Fading
- Losing Ground
- Slipping Back

There's more. Try these for size:

- Cracked
- Drab and dingy
- Frayed
- Moth-eaten
- Mouldering
- Seedy
- Tatty
- Tottery
- Worn to a Frazzle
- Worse for Wear

These quotations from Roget may prompt nightmares, indigestion and palpitations, even suggesting with more than just a hint of menace that as your vital life force fades, all those juices that once coursed through your body with a manic zest will now turn sour and flow sluggishly like rancid butter. Furthermore, your skin will coarsen, crack, flake and blister, your gums will shrink and your teeth, if not already loose with decay, will develop a yellowish glaze. Your tongue will fur, your nasal passages will fill with toxic mucus, your heartbeat will become irregular, nails and fingertips will split, toes will curl, belly will sag, eyes will fill with rheum, nerve ends will twitch and tremble, sending electric screams through your rotting, sinking, sagging, suppurating hulk of a body that will signal accelerating decrepitude and system collapse.

Are you still with me? Good, because there's still more. Your breath could become a fetid, corpse-like stench and the very skeleton on which hangs this drooping, wheezing, calcifying envelope of flesh and organs will creak and change shape, like a stricken oak in a thunderstorm.

And in the theatre of your imagination, you will be attended by gargoyles, pall-bearers, hunchbacks, demons and gravediggers. Doubt and terror in equal measure will rain down to pound your mind, body and spirit as the death's head, a scythe shouldered on his bony clavicle, leeringly beckons.

On the other hand, you might wish to ignore these ravings (I blame Roget) and consider the alternative, fluffy vision of yourself in retirement. Silver-haired and avuncular, you stride hand in hand with your partner over springy turf beneath an azure sky. Your skin is clear, those wrinkles around your eyes are no more than laughter lines, your teeth gleam with an ethereal light and all your organs are functioning slowly, but well. There is no hint of lameness in your gait, no demons visit your dreams and the soundness of your heart and spirit suggest you have at least a decade more of well-earned enjoyment on the golf course, the cruise ship and the palm-fringed beach still ahead of you.

Let's be blunt. If we are lucky enough to have survived into an age where we have actually retired, and are still more or less in one piece, we are entering a phase of our life, probably the last phase, for which we have had no training, no rehearsal and absolutely no idea of how to handle it.

The purpose of this little book, therefore, is to provide a short but random guide of not just what you should do in retirement to achieve

minimum happiness, but what you should avoid – like the plague …
particularly the plague.

If you don't like home truths or are excessively PC, don't read on.
You've wasted your money. This book will only upset you. Stop right here.
Sorry. For the rest of you still reading, sit back, loosen your clothing, put
your teeth in a glass on a table next to you and read on, slowly, but try to
avoid moving your lips at the same time, it looks so senile.

A

Advertising

As an ex-vice chairman of the British Advertising Association, I have a clear view of the role that advertising plays in our modern society. But as an old-age pensioner, I believe my take on the ad business is very similar to yours. In other words, while accepting it as a part of the kaleidoscope of free market enterprise and a tool to inform, persuade and sell, it is also, particularly to us oldies, a source of irritation and occasional bafflement. This is primarily because most advertising, certainly on television, is aimed at young consumers.

The grey market, i.e. you and I, is rarely addressed and when it is, the tone is likely to be patronising. We must accept this with a patient shrug, as the copywriters, art directors and TV producers who toil in the lush pastures of the advertising agencies are themselves mostly young, hip, turned-on, research-fed and market driven.

But mass advertising is now a hugely powerful force in most modern societies. It is all-embracing, intrusive, entertaining (sometimes), dazzling and, of course, persuasive. Politicians, even those who abhor the raw capitalistic culture that advertising is such an integral part of, still use advertising to promote themselves and their particular policies.

The sheer volume of commercial messages we are all exposed to on a daily basis is enormous. It is estimated that Americans are exposed to over 3,000 messages every day, radio, posters, TV ads, buses, taxis and much else besides. In Britain, we are the target of a similar bombardment of seduction, wheedling, cajoling, persuading and informing. There are large screen videos in public squares, alongside motorways, in tube trains and retail stores. Waiting rooms, pubs, airport departure lounges and railway stations. Slogans urging us to buy appear on everyday objects from knives to the clothes we wear, so that some people in leisure gear appear as human sandwich boards. The result of this tidal wave of advertising is a sensory glut and an overload of information that can and does lead to a diminution of impact.

For older people, we find it easier to blot out the firestorm of messages that are sweeping over us each day. With age comes discrimination and we are more able than younger people to reject or ignore that which is not relevant to us.

In the sixties, seventies and eighties, when I earned my living in the world of television advertising, there were certain golden rules about advertisements. A 'good' advertisement was one that persuaded you to buy the product or service on offer or at least remember the brand in a positive light, so that on your next shopping expedition you would choose it over it rivals. But the building blocks of a good advertisement are timeless. To judge whether an advertisement you have just seen is 'good' or 'bad', ask yourself the following questions:

1. Did I remember the name of the product or service on offer?

2. Did the advertisement give me a compelling reason to want to purchase the product or service?

3. Did the clever camera work, music track and slick editing detract from the core message?

4. Am I likely to remember the selling proposition (i.e. why I should purchase or rent the item on offer)?

5. Did the advertisement have a solid ring of truth?

Yes, I know, you have seen dozens of commercials in which the actual product being advertised is obscure, sometimes invisible, and there is no rational reason given for anybody, especially you, to purchase it. But the 'grey' market is a growing market and a pretty lucrative one, too.

Although it is booming in America, one service that has not reached Britain yet is an 'Advance Burial Package', where you can book your plot, pick your coffin and even specify the music and flowers you might like on that special day. Some of the American TV ads offering this service are so toe-curlingly twee as to make you spill your mug of Horlicks while you're watching. Cheer up though; I don't think their arrival on British TV screens is imminent.

There is one final piece of advice from an old ad-man and it may surprise you. If an advertisement, in print or on television, annoys or patronises you – do not buy the product. Switch brands. The really good advertising manager or their agent will welcome feedback and the most potent feedback is whether their product is flying off the shelves or just sitting there like a virgin at an orgy. Happy viewing, folks.

Quick Quote:

I find TV advertising

very educational. Every

time an advert appears

on my screen, I go into

another room and read

a book.

Groucho Marx

Advice and Adversity

Once you retire, the bombardment by companies wishing to sell you vitamin pills, stairlifts, trusses, incontinence pants, burial plots, nasal sprays, Viagra, conversion to Islam, fruit cake, dance lessons, winter cruises, bowling club membership, basket weaving classes, home-visiting masseurs, tins of calves-foot jelly, monogrammed toothpicks, fleece-lined slippers with little bobbles and a host of other, largely useless junk, reaches blitz proportions.

However much you resolve not to be seduced by these commercial blandishments, you will eventually succumb. Usually to some product or service that relates to your health or longevity. This is just vanity on your part. A triumph of hope over experience.

Most doctors now admit that provided you eat a balanced diet, the need for the myriad of vitamin supplements on the market is largely redundant. I looked in my bathroom cabinet the other day and noted, with a stab of desperation, that I have more bottles of stuff than you could shake a stick at. I had pills to alleviate brittle bones, pills to cleanse my blood, pills to sharpen my eyesight, pills to overcome tiredness, pills to help keep my arteries from furring up, vitamins A, B, C, D, E, and Z, pills to act as a diuretic, painkillers, pick-me-ups, sore throat remedies, corn removing liquid, nail strengtheners, eye drops, small jelly capsules, which I assume you either swallow or stick up your bum – I've tried both, they both have the same effect, zero – plus medicated plasters, moisturising cream, ear drops, toenail fungus treatments, haemorrhoid cream, lactose intolerance gel, indigestion tablets, wart remover, athlete's foot powder, diarrhoeic pills, constipation tablets (important not to mix these up, could be socially embarrassing) and little pamphlets offering five ideas for getting rid of gas, several slim books offering detailed advice on irritable bowel syndrome, intermittent causation, laryngitis, osteoporosis, hang nails, genital herpes, eye strain, blisters, body odour, boils and bruxism (that's grinding your teeth). I did a lot of teeth grinding when I added up what I'd spent on this accumulation of junk, which frankly is what most of it is.

Therefore, apart from any pill or potion actually prescribed by your physician, the only thing you should consider ingesting each morning after your cornflakes is:

a. An Aspirin

b. A fish oil tablet

Honestly, that's about it. Think of the money you'll save on all that other stuff. You might even be able to take up smoking again. Or hang-gliding.

Ageing

You may hate the idea of growing older, but just think of the alternative. Ageing, therefore, should be a cause for celebration. However, always add nine years to your actual birth date; this will produce ego-boosting responses like 'my goodness, you don't look it'. It doesn't matter if the person saying this utters the words through gritted teeth, they will have said it. And at your age a bit of flattery goes a long way.

Anecdotes

Old people like telling anecdotes, but they are usually boring, especially to friends and relatives who are politely obliged to listen to them. If you are a boring anecdotalist – you *are*, aren't you? – here's what to do: don't just exaggerate, make them up. Lie shamelessly. Spin the most ridiculous stories you can think of. There is a golden rule about anecdotes, particularly at dinner parties – they don't have to be true, but they have to be amusing. But keep them short.

For example, if you've spent thirty-eight years in an exceedingly boring job, like accountancy or nail varnish design, telling the truth about your life will drive people to sleep, or insane, so don't do it. Pretend the job was just a cover for your real activities as any of the following:

1. A transvestite hypnotist

2. The voice for the speaking clock in Bulgaria

3. The author of four books on cannibalism in Budleigh Salterton

4. An axe murderer

> **Quick Quote:**
>
> My financial advisor said I had
>
> enough money in my savings to
>
> live in total luxury for the rest
>
> my life – provided I died in two
>
> years time.
>
> Anon

Armpits

Old people's armpits are seldom charm-pits. Shave them. And use a deodorant. Daily. Not a spray; with your eyesight you'll probably miss and blind the cat. Use a roll-on.

Art

Whatever your taste, never criticise modern art, not even Tracey Emin's. Young people expect you to grumble and say, 'It's horrible'. Instead, say, 'How profound it is' – how so 'in' and 'how you see the artist's hidden agenda'.

Stuff like this will really piss young people off. They hate it if they think they share your taste. They'll switch to Constable just to spite you.

Arthritis (Inflammation of the Joints)

You're old; chances are you'll have a touch of arthritis. It's all part of the ageing process and while the most common type is osteoarthritis, the really nasty one is rheumatoid arthritis, which in its extreme form can be a crippling disease.

However, osteoarthritis often hits the finger joints and tends to flare up in damp or cold weather. I have a touch of it in my hands and occasionally my feet but, luckily, it is sporadic and I am not overly troubled by its sneaky attacks.

I can offer no advice to rheumatoid arthritis sufferers, who must rely on proper medical supervision, but I can suggest a few tips for those of you with mild osteoarthritis:

1. If you are overweight, this will place an extra strain on your joints – so lose it.

2. Choose mild exercises to keep one flexible and avoid jogging or other jarring activities.

3. When swelling occurs, apply cold packs for relief; never heat.

4. If you take an anti-inflammatory medicine such as Aspirin or Ibuprofen, don't combine them.

5. If you are out in the rain and you get your feet wet or, indeed, any other part of your body, avoid staying in damp clothes for a moment longer than necessary. Wet clothes that are allowed to dry on you while you are wearing them are a sure way to encourage osteoarthritis.

That's about all I can offer on this subject, but if you think you've developed a touch of osteo, you must tell your doctor. I know old people don't like 'bothering doctors unnecessarily', but you really must. No funny quips in this section, folks, because arthritis is no laughing matter.

I can recommend the anti-inflammatory cream Ibuleve. It works for me, giving temporary relief, but don't use it if you are taking Ibuprofen.

PS I lied. Here's one:

An old man shuffled into an ice-cream parlour and ordered a banana split.

'Crushed nuts?' asked the waitress.

'No,' said the old fellow, 'arthritis.'

Aspirin

Yes, the humble Aspirin. It is in my opinion something of a miracle drug. Over many years, it has proved to be reliable, effective and safe. I take a very small one every day, as did my mother before me. Old people should never be without a bottle of Aspirin in their bathroom cabinet. It can work just as well for a headache as some of the more expensive products on the market.

OK. 'Elf and Safety' will no doubt purse their lips and wag a finger while muttering, 'don't overdose, this can cause stomach bleeding'. We did know that, us old folk. We also know that Aspirin is best taken just after eating and with a glass of water. If you are an Aspirin taker, however, it's best not to swallow one with citrus fruits or fruit juice, as this can increase stomach irritation. Though, most Aspirins you buy at a good chemist will have an enteric coating, which delays the absorption of Aspirin until it reaches your intestine.

When I was in the army, an officer colleague of mine used to make himself an Aspirin sandwich in the morning after a night of alcoholic excess. This treat consisted of two doorstep slices of white bread, heavily buttered, and half a dozen baby Aspirins, which he pressed between the slices, but in spite of such boasts, I don't think it is something old people should try at home.

Aviation

If you fly, particularly on long-haul flights, book aisle seats. Why? Well, on a trip to New York, for example, you will need to get up and have a pee eight times and there is nothing more irritating to other passengers than an incontinent wrinkly constantly clambering over them from the centre seat with a strained expression on their face. Avoid those air-filled plastic pants you can by on eBay. At certain altitudes, they tend to explode. Need I say more?

Accept that the Mile High Club is not for anybody over twenty-one, overweight or who wears cream-coloured Y-fronts that have a waistband that reaches just below the chest.

B

Back Pain

'Back pain,' my old father used to say, 'is a pain in the butt.' Except he didn't. I just made that up to catch your attention, in case you were drifting. But even if my dad didn't utter those words, back pain is one of the most complained about conditions among the over 65-year-olds.

Part of the ageing process, of course, but it's worth remembering the structure of the human frame, with a spine running down the centre of the back, is not really conducive to walking upright. Surely, we should be on all fours, where we would not be throwing such a strain on our skeletal and muscular framework. Though, that is obviously quite impractical, in spite of the geometry being more or less correct.

Now, if you have a severe back problem, you are probably under doctor's orders already, but if, however, your back pain is just mild and nagging, there are a few steps you can take to alleviate the situation:

1. Don't stay sitting or standing in the same position for long periods while working.

2. Sleep on a firm mattress. Those squishy jobs are silent killers.

3. Use a pillow that doesn't elevate your head too much. This will crimp your neck and spread to your upper back.

4. Forget high heels. Yes, you men, too. The higher the heel the more chance of back pain.

5. Avoid lifting heavy objects. On those occasions when it is unavoidable, keep your back straight, bend the knees and push with your legs. If you've ever seen Olympic weightlifting on television, you will have observed that the athletes always heave up those massive poundages as much with a drive of their legs as with their arms.

6. Always push a heavy item. Never pull it. If you do, you'll hear and feel that fatal 'ping' as your back goes. So don't do it. Always push or, better still, get somebody else to shift the bloody thing!

7. In bed, lie on your side and draw your knees up towards your chin. This is known as the foetal position. So back to the womb, Grandad, you know it makes sense.

8. Lose weight. A beer gut on men puts a great strain on the back. If you refuse to give up your eight pints of wallop a night, then try wearing a corset and back belt, to give your poor old back support.

9. Posture. Stand up straight. Even when sitting down. Crazy? Not really. Slumping like a sack of rotting artichokes on that comfy sofa will have you ending up looking like the Hunchback of Notre Dame.

10. Finally, as cops always say in American movies when confronting a crook – 'Don't make any sudden moves'. Move smoothly, without jerking. You can do that, Grandma, can't you?

Look after your back. You've only one and it's got to last a lifetime.

> Quick Quote:
>
> Anyone can get old.
>
> All you have to
>
> do is live long
>
> enough.
>
> Groucho Marx

The BBC

Yes, dear Old Auntie. And why, you may ask with a petulant shrug, is The British Broadcasting Corporation included in a book that purports to define the Gentle Art of Retirement? Well, simple, really. The BBC is a very old British thing. Rather like you and me, actually. And like you it sometimes gives the impression of not knowing quite how to cope with the fast-moving trends in modern life.

This said, in spite of its tendency to cast off the lace-trimmed shawl of conventions and cavort in a miniskirt and stilettos, it is still a remarkable and uniquely British institution. Older people tend to watch the BBC rather than the myriad of commercial and satellite channels and the same preference is shown for BBC radio over the frenetic offerings from the glut of advertising-led radio stations, both local and national.

So let's get to the heart of what I'm rattling on about. There is talk, quite serious talk, of the BBC being sold off and being forced to earn its keep in the scary world of competition. At present, the Beeb survives on a not-so-subtle form of compulsory taxation. If you own a TV set, you pay the licence fee. Apart from the over seventy-fives, of course. So how should we, the oldies, react to these suggestions that Auntie should be privatised?

Before reaching a conclusion, if you haven't already done so, try this on for size. The BBC is unique in as much as it provides both the best and the worst in both visual and radio broadcasting. It tries, because of its remit, to be all things to all men – and women. Sometimes it succeeds, but often it fails. It is very touchy about criticism. Like an ageing prima donna, it rebuffs any attack with a silvery laugh and a coquettish turn of the head. It is a gigantic bureaucracy. It is incestuous and overstaffed with non-creative managers.

It can and does, however, occasionally produce programmes of staggering brilliance and originality. And its World Service is without parallel. But its news and current affairs are increasingly tainted by political correctness and a tendency to favour the soft, liberal left. It claims to present balanced political views, which are frequently open to question.

It overpays some of its creative people obscene amounts of money, which in a public company would have the shareholders in revolt. So why not privatise it and save all those licence-payers oodles of money? I earned my living for thirty years in the world of commercial television and the BBC was my competitor, at least in programme terms.

So am I in favour of pitching Auntie, kicking and screaming, into the fierce world of competition, advertising and sponsorship? Well, actually, no. I am in favour of retaining the licence fee and keeping the BBC independent of both government intervention and commercialism. However, as I am urging all of you oldies out there to support the role of the BBC, just as I do, there are a few caveats and more than a few 'ifs' and 'buts'. Maybe you'll agree with them. First and foremost, the BBC should cut out and abandon the proliferating range of activities it now indulges in. At its TV core should be BBC 1, BBC 2 and *no more*. No BBC 3, no fancy kids' channels, no silly interactive nonsense and ethnic 'cringe' speciality channels. Just BBC 1 and BBC 2.

As far as radio is concerned, 1, 2 and 4, particularly 4, should be retained, along with the magnificent World Service, and no more. If the current licence fee, which guarantees the BBC a vast income, were utilised only to fund these radio and television channels, they could return to their roots, planted long ago by the now reviled Lord Reith, and provide programmes that would: educate, inform and entertain. That's what a publicly funded BBC should be doing.

One other thing: the money should be directed to creative output, not useless, meeting-obsessed, paper-pushing middle management. If fifty per cent of non-productive (i.e. non-creative staff) were fired overnight, I doubt if it would make a halfpence of difference to the quality of what you see on your screens or listen to on your radios. It might even lead to some improvement.

So to all of you old BBC viewers and listeners, may I conclude by saying this: support Dear Auntie, but only if she refrains from lurching into the trendy, the excruciatingly fashionable and the tendency to confuse technical innovations with solid creativity.

So write to Auntie, politely and firmly make your opinions clear and with a bit of luck, poor old Lord Reith will stop spinning in his grave.

Bedsores

Another horrid subject. But old people do tend to suffer from bedsores and not always when they are bedridden.

My doctor's tips for avoiding bedsores are:

1. Vitamin 'C': take up to 500mg of vitamin C a day.

2. Use of inflated rubber cushions helps to avoid bedsores. (Sounds a bit kinky to me.)

3. Keep bedclothes loose.

My advice to avoid bedsores 100 per cent? Don't go to bed. Try sleeping while standing up or buy a hammock.

Belgium

It is not really a country and should not be on any old-age pensioner's list of places to visit. It used to be called The Spanish Netherlands and the only excuse for passing through is if you fancy walking over the old battlefield of Waterloo. Here, you will find, in the souvenir shop adjoining the battlefield, lots of plaster busts of Napoleon and little statues of his horse Marengo. I have been three times and I have never been able to find a bust of Wellington (see 'W' for Duke of Wellington) who, after all, won the Battle of Waterloo. Whereas Napoleon lost.

Oh alright, Brussels is a fine city with some spectacular restaurants, but that's about it. Sorry. And Hercule Poirot is not a real person. Belgian chocolates are OK, though.

Quick Quote:

I'm at an age where

my back goes out

more than I do.

Phyllis Diller

Bidets

The little porcelain job you now find in most classy hotel bathrooms. And some modern homes. When I was a lad, nobody had ever heard of a bidet. When I first encountered one, I was about fourteen. I thought it was a little toilet for midget guests, children or dogs.

No research has ever been done as far as I am aware as to how many hotel guests actually use the damn things. My guess is that most people ignore them or just put their toiletry bags in them. But Americans use them. Of course they do. Far more than we Europeans. Why? Don't even go there.

Many years ago, the film star Shirley MacLaine was staying at an unmodernised hotel in either Germany, France or England, I can't remember where, and was shocked to find there was no bidet in her bathroom. Legend has it that she phoned her friend Frank Sinatra in Palm Springs, USA, and bemoaned the situation in which she found herself. 'No bidet, Frank!' she cried in horror. 'No bidet!'

Sinatra's reply was succinct. 'Don't worry, Shirley; just do a handstand in the shower.'

Bottoms

These should be concealed at all times. On the beach, never wear a thong (see 'C' for Clothes), or Bermuda shorts. (In California, elderly thong wearers have been shot dead by specially trained marksmen.) Long, Victorian woollen bathing suits with shoulder straps are the best choice. Remember, no buttock should ever be seen if it is more than 49 and a half years old, except by a nurse, provided she wears dark glasses and a gauze mask.

Bowels

Oh alright, I'll be brief. But bowels are jolly important things, especially in us oldies.

Doctors frequently urge us to 'keep them open' as if they were a pair of swings doors. Bowels, of course, are part of that extraordinary factory system inside our bodies, which includes the stomach, intestines and lots of other slippery bits.

So how best to avoid the dreaded constipation that plagues so many of us in later years? Diet is important: fibre, fruit, greens and other vegetables are helpful. Vindaloo curry may be a quick fix, but I don't recommend it for long-term success. Your local chemist will almost certainly stock a variety of products which can help, but my own doctor suggests if you follow sensible diet rules, you shouldn't need them. And do try and 'go' regularly at the same time each morning.

Routine, my doctor says, is crucial, together with drinking at least eight glasses of water a day. Yes – water. This is not *instead* of your evening noggin or wine at dinner, but in *addition* to it. So not only will this consumption of Adam's Ale help you to perform on the loo, but it will flush through your system and kidneys and prevent you from dehydrating which, I am reliably informed, is a condition commonly found in elderly people.

So that's it then. Just wack into the fruit, fibre and veggies, swig eight glasses of water, hit the porcelain at the same time every day and you will enjoy, God willing, 'Happy Bowel Syndrome'.

Breakfast

This is the most important meal in the whole day for old people. Make it substantial – even gargantuan – and it won't matter if you miss lunch and if your evening meal is a light snack.

Doctors agree with the old saw – breakfast like a king, dine like a pauper. So whack into the cornflakes, bacon, eggs, toast, mushrooms, tomatoes and almost anything else that comes to hand, including potatoes. This meal, regularly taken, could be your ticket to an even longer and more vital life than you've had so far.

And yes – take a glass of champagne with it if your budget runs this far or maybe a beer. Brown ale or Guinness, rather than a gassy lager. And instead of coffee, try tea – with no milk – and, of course, orange juice for your vitamin C.

Try a big breakfast – really big – for a month and Dr Harry believes you will feel a new surge of life and energy.

Bruises

Old people bruise easily. When I worked as a volunteer in my local hospital, I saw elderly patients who looked as if they had been bounced off walls, so covered were they with big blue and black bruises.

Bruises occur when small blood vessels in the soft tissue under the skin break. The bruise mark turns blue, before going yellow as the leak is gradually repaired by the body's process.

Old people can bruise with the slightest knock, not just heavy falls. If you are susceptible to bruising, you can strengthen the capillary walls to some extent with vitamin C. Foods rich in 'C' include fruit and berries, cabbage, green vegetables and potatoes. (I'm so glad about potatoes. I love them.) Zinc, too, can help people who bruise easily. If all else fails, you could try wearing a Mr Blobby suit; then you could bounce all over the house to your heart's content without hurting yourself.

C

Call Centres

The very words 'call centres' have the ability to conjure within me a veritable firestorm of howling rage, a gibbering, incoherent fury, a massive elevation in blood pressure and a maniacal tic in my right eye that is invariably accompanied by a wholly irrational desire to defecate in my hat and run naked down the high street, sobbing like a scalded infant.

All of the aforementioned, of course, cuts absolutely no mustard with the call centre itself. This is because a call centre is not staffed by humans but by mechanical androids, specially selected by a vicious gang of wealthy thugs, whose sole purpose is to kill you.

'OK, calm down, dear, it's only a commercial.' (My wife wrote that.)

Alright already. Call centres are here to stay, a fact of modern life, and we oldies have to face it fair and square. So, here's a few tips, many of which I have ignored myself, but regularly resolve to employ next time I am hanging onto the phone in a white-knuckled rage and being told that either 'the computer has broken down' or 'all the specialist staff who can help you are engaged and you are in a queue'.

Don'ts:

1. Shout

2. Raise your voice

3. Ask how the weather is in Delhi today

4. Slam the phone down (they can't hear you)

Do's

1. Breathe deeply

2. Remain icy calm

3. Remember to write down all the relevant information you may need before you make the call

4. Thank the person (or android) profusely when they finally provide the answer or solution you are seeking

I was going to mention British Telecom, whose slogan is 'It's good to talk', but as it is impossible ever to talk to a human being at BT, only a machine, I won't mention them. If I do mention them, it will only make me very ill, so I won't; no, really, I will not mention BT ever again. Ever.

> **Quick Quote:**
>
> My bank has 160
>
> people working at
>
> its Call Centre
>
> except when it's
>
> busy – then they
>
> have 12.
>
> Anon

Cardigans

It's truly amazing that this simple woollen garment, named after the foolhardy but gallant Lord Cardigan, who led the famous Charge of the Light Brigade in the Crimean War, has become exclusively associated with old people. The problem, I think, is misuse. Let me explain. A new woollen cardigan is purchased by your typical octogenarian or maybe given to them as a present. It is designed to be worn casually about the house, along with slippers and – in smarter circles – a cravat as well. But not content with donning this cosy item, your 80-year-old then stuffs each of the two side pockets full of geriatric-style junk.

You know the sort of stuff. Tins of tobacco, loose change, boxes of matches (always Swan Vestas), nasal inhalers, bottles of Aspirin, pairs of sexy knickers that have been thrown at him by a crazed woman pensioner while he performed karaoke at the local Darby and Joan Christmas piss-up. Once in their pockets, this stuff is never removed. As old people's cardigans are also never laundered or dry cleaned, the junk piles up, getting heavier and heavier, until the pockets bulge and sag and the weight of the bottles, tobacco, coins, knickers, filthy handkerchiefs, dead sparrows, fluff, lucky rabbits' feet, half-eaten toffees and shrunken Pygmy heads exert a downward pull on the whole garment, until it hangs unevenly below the knees.

To accommodate this gravitational inevitability, the wearer adopts a stooping posture, which soon becomes permanent, and they will rapidly transmogrify into an uncanny imitation of Quasimodo, Victor Hugo's Hunchback of Notre Dame.

So the advice to all cardigan wearers of advanced years is to: stand up straight, get your wife to sew the bloody pockets up and open a monthly account at the local dry cleaners.

Quick Quote

An old bachelor friend of mine

never takes his clothes to the

dry cleaners or the laundry.

When he undresses at night,

he just props them upright

against the wall.

Causes of Death

What a morbid subject. I recently read of the ten leading causes of death in America; my doctor says it is probably very similar in this country. They are:

1. Heart disease

2. Cancer

3. Stroke

4. Accidents

5. Lung disease

6. Pneumonia and influenza

7. Diabetes

8. Cirrhosis of the liver

9. Circulatory disease

10. Suicide

Total rubbish. The leading cause of death in every country in the world is stopping breathing. Remember, you read it here first.

China

Try to visit China. Old people are revered there. But don't expect to enjoy the food. It may look like what you get at the Green Dragon Takeaway in Penge, but in China, it tastes like a cross-country runner's jockstrap.

Chips

Old people can exist on a diet consisting entirely of chips. Yes, they can. The Irish did until the potato famine. Avoid reading the 'Health Pages' of the *Daily Mail*, which keeps banging on about how old people should have 'balanced diets'. All you need to know about balance is how to balance a big dish of hot chips on your lap while watching television. And after the age of seventy-five, you don't have to pay the licence fee.

Start lobbying immediately for free chips for pensioners and your life will be complete.

Quick Quote

When you're old, if you drink

a glass of sulphuric acid, neat,

you'll get chronic indigestion

and flatulence long before you die.

Gaylord Weston

Choice

In the lifetime of most old people, the amount and variety of choice available to them is quite staggering. In shops and restaurants and in choosing holidays, houses, cars and clothes, there exists a cornucopia of choice, a veritable Horn of Plenty, disgorging all the treasures of a vastly wealthy consumer society.

Choice means competition and vice versa, creating a virtuous circle of benefit to us all. Or so we are told. But is this really true?

Most people accept that the goodies on offer in our fast-moving, faintly manic way of life are a vast improvement on what was available when we were growing up. But I detect a note of caution in the conversations I have had with older people, both when I worked in the world of television advertising and since I have myself become part of the 'grey' consumer market.

Is there such a thing as too much choice? Do we need umpteen different brands of vinegar or double-umpteen cans of baked beans? On television, the proliferation of channels has really only provided more of the same. All this, the shrewd marketing man will tell you, leads to 'information overload', which is a very bad thing.

I doubt if we can turn the clock back and deny all these bushy tailed and eager new products and services entry to the rich but overcrowded consumer marketplace. But I have a particular bugbear (and yes, I know the word bugbear dates me, but what the hell), when I am dispatched by my wife to do a little light shopping at our local supermarket.

On my list of items, I am under pain of the lash to obtain would-be breakfast cereal and potato crisps. When I glide up to the display that carries either of these delectable items, I am at once presented with the dreaded 'information overload'. I am seeking cornflakes and potato crisps, which is what I want. What is on offer, however, are cornflakes with dried fruit, cornflakes with honey, cornflakes with little chocolate bits, cornflakes with powdered rhinoceros horn – OK, that's a mild exaggeration but, dear reader, you catch the nub of my drift?

I do eventually locate the plain and simple Cornflakes packet, which lurks shamefacedly at the back of the shelf. But, by now, my brain is hurting. Same thing with the crisps. Oh yes. Of course, there are plain bags of crisps, but they are surrounded by crisps flavoured with just about everything from vinegar to cheese and onion.

Are our tastes becoming so jaded that even the most basic foodstuffs have to be adulterated with all these trivial bits and pieces? I think old people should press for greater simplicity in foodstuffs and a return to basics.

I don't know about you, but these days a visit to the supermarket requires so many decisions about so many products that I can't wait to finish the shopping and go home for a stiff drink, just to clear my head. Problem is, should it be Scotch whisky, Irish whisky, Japanese whisky, Famous Grouse, Dewar's, Black and White, Sainsbury's own or that gut-rot you brewers illegally brew in the old galvanised dustbin in the garden shed? The choice is yours. Or is it mine?

Choking

We are not talking here about what you want to do to certain other people who insist on yammering nineteen to the dozen in a shrill voice when you are watching your favourite programme on television.

What we are talking about is the nasty business of choking when you are an old person alone in the house. This can be a frightening experience, either when a cough goes wrong or when you swallow something and it sticks in your throat.

Here's what to do:

1. Put your fist against your stomach just below the rib cage.

2. Grab your fist with the other hand and give it an upwards thrust, while pressing hard against your stomach.

3. Repeat till that bit of toast is expelled or properly swallowed.

This is called the Heimlich Manoeuvre. Yes, it is. Trust me. It's not what a German tank commander did to avoid Montgomery's frontal attack at El Alamein. It was invented by a mad scientist called Dr Henry Heimlich. OK, he wasn't mad. But many scientists are. They wouldn't be scientists if they weren't, would they? It stands to reason. Oh yes, you can perform the Heimlich Manoeuvre standing up, sitting down or lying down.

On second thoughts, he was mad.

Quick Quote:

Some mornings, it's

just not worth

chewing through the

leather straps.

Emo Philips

Clothes

How you dress when you are old may not be the most urgent thing
on your checklist, but it is worth finding time to rummage through
your wardrobe to see whether that Hawaiian shirt, frilly frock or
double-breasted suit really deserve to stay there or be handed over –
clean and pressed – to the local Oxfam shop and yes, you must be
ruthless! Remember, it is other people who have to observe you
when you emerge from home to saunter down to the post office to
collect your pension. So dress for your age and don't try to compete
with all those 45-year-olds, who are still trying to kid themselves they
are only twenty.

While how you dress when old is very much a personal thing, here are
a few general dos and don'ts which, I venture to suggest, will, if followed,
prevent you from making too many sartorial blunders. Don't wear:

- Anything that shows your knees, even in summer
- A shirt or blouse unbuttoned at the throat, unless accompanied
  by a cravat or scarf. (It's those turtle-like wrinkles you need to
  mask.)
- Trainers, (especially those with little lights in the heel)
- Baseball caps
- Stetsons
- Pointed Ku Klux Klan hats
- T-shirts with rude slogans, i.e. 'That Person Next To Me Is Pissed'
- Floral-print frocks. Yes, really, they are so 'old' looking and even
  worse on men
- Cream Y-fronts (for men)

- Bloomers with elastic just above the knee (for women)
- Thongs (see 'B' for Bottoms)
- Woolly cardigans (unless confined to indoor wear)
- Shell suits (Ugh!)

Do Wear:

- Clothes that are regularly cleaned and pressed
- Pastel shades or grey (but black is OK for formal occasions)
- Clothes that fit
- Wool and cotton rather than nylon
- Long-sleeved shirts or blouses (those old elbows and flabby upper arms again!)
- Self-supporting socks
- Highly polished leather footwear

Not an exhaustive list I will concede, but it should point you in the right direction unless, of course, you are one of those obstinate old codgers who revel in looking like a homeless tramp.

Finally, if you haven't already got one, invest in a full-length mirror and it is much better to spot that unbuttoned fly or wrinkled stocking before you leave the house, rather than suffer the embarrassment of seeing your reflection in a shop window in the high street.

Quick Quote:

An old man walked into an Army

Surplus Store and asked if they

had any camouflage trousers.

'Yes, we have,' said the equally

ancient sales assistant, 'but we

can't find them.'

Commission for Racial Equality (CRE)

Old people may be surprised to hear that the CRE was set up by the government to monitor breaches of the Race Relations Act and to promote racial harmony between the different racial groups in our country. A good thing surely? Certainly; then why are so many old people surprised at my description of CRE?

They are surprised (like me), because they rather suspect this noble-sounding organisation really exists to stifle free speech and punish transgressors, who stray from the rigid path of politically correct speech patterns they themselves have set.

Do I exaggerate? Just a little? Am I guilty of a soupçon of hyperbole? I think not. Just consider this: in 2007, a man was threatened with prosecution because, while objecting to the illegal siting of a group of caravans in his village, he described the caravan dwellers as 'itinerant travellers'.

If that, dear readers, is a racist remark, then I am a roller-skating nun. Onslaughts on the freedom of speech like this are happening on a regular basis in our country. Old people who have developed speech patterns and methods of address over many years, wholly innocent of offensive intent, are now being treated like pariahs by the zealots who now infest quangos like the CRE and other similar groups. So what are we to do in the face of such assaults?

While we may have to accept that some old-fashioned epithets are now taboo, we must not allow the thought and race police to purge our speech of all its richness and yes – its bawdiness. We must continue to use the phrases, compliments and good-natured insults that have added many colourful threads to the great tapestry of our language over the last decades. Our good sense will tell us what is unacceptable or hurtful to others. We don't need a bunch of purse-lipped, taxpayer-funded pecksniffians threatening us with legal sanction if we cross the arbitrary boundaries that they lay down.

In a society where all political parties seem bent on exercising control over every aspect of our lives, remember that our most precious freedom is freedom of speech, under the law, and that this freedom, once curbed or tampered with, leads down a slippery slope to perdition. Old people should realise that this is a clear and present danger and that it is our responsibility to our children to ensure that this freedom is not stifled either by stealth or by decree.

Computers

The elderly fall into three broad categories as far as computers are concerned. There are those who take to emailing and surfing the

Internet like ducks to water, usually encouraged by their children or grandchildren. I suspect they are in the minority.

Then there are the refuseniks (one of which I used to be). The group who stubbornly resist all attempts to wean them into the terrifying world of cyberspace. This group is often called the 'Quill Pen Brigade'. They prefer to communicate by telephone, which their grandparents probably shied away from, or by letter.

Finally, there are the 'Late Converted' and yes, I am one of these now. However, a word of caution to those of you who are about to chuck away your quill pen and squat in front of that seductive little screen. Don't get hooked. Use the computer for specific tasks that you decide. Fix your priorities and stick to them. Don't become a computer anorak and waste hours in front of the wretched thing. And avoid anything that claims to be 'virtual reality'. The phrase itself is almost an oxymoron.

It is a cause of great sadness and concern that today, many young people prefer to communicate socially by email or texting rather than face-to-face. Virtual reality is a con. There is no substitute for personal, human contact. 'Email' your grandchildren by all means, but this will never replace giving them a hug or even hearing their voices on the telephone.

Internet shopping? EBay and the rest of it? Well, that is a matter of personal choice but, as far as I am concerned, I wouldn't buy anything off a screen that I couldn't touch, taste or smell. And I would hesitate to commit credit or debit card details to cyberspace. The very thought of it makes the two plastic cards in my wallet curl up at the edges.

So use the computer, but don't let it use you.

Quick Quote:

No matter how twisted

a sexual pervert you are,

the web will introduce

you to thousands of friends

of a like mind. Type in

'Find people who only

have sex with goats that

are on fire' and the

computer will say

'Specify precise type

of goat'.

Anon

Coughing

Come on, admit it. Old people cough. They cough first thing in the morning when they get up. They cough in trains, they hack and hawk in supermarkets and they release a series of short, barking noises in the theatre, when you are about to enjoy a performance of *The Importance of Being Earnest* by Oscar Wilde. (You know who you are, Grandad, and I know where you live!) Some old people cough politely behind their hands. Others tear out coughs like the death cry of a wounded Cape buffalo.

Coughing, however, is a perfectly natural thing. It is the body's way of getting foreign substances and mucus out of the respiratory system. But there is a world of difference between the occasional cough and the serial hacker.

There are, of course, countless cough remedies on the market you can suck, swallow or inhale, but before you spend money, if you are troubled by a persistent cough, try a drink of lemon and honey in a glass of hot water. It works for me. But if all else fails, including everything a good chemist has to offer, go and see your doctor and go soon, before that bloke sitting behind you in the theatre beats you unconscious with the heel of his shoe.

Creeds (Political)

We have touched on politics generally under another heading, but it is worth looking specifically at some of the formulated beliefs older people hold, as they tend to be more robust than those of the young or middle aged. Indeed, some older people's beliefs are described as being dogmatic, inflexible or plain stubborn.

Personally, I think old people's political beliefs, or articles of faith, are often sewn into their subconscious when they are quite young. There is even a school of thought that implies that our genes are responsible for which side of the political spectrum we finally end up with. Who knows?

So what's it all about, folks? Are we dyed-in-the-wool Tories, socialists, Liberals or simply political neutrals, who wish a plague on all their houses? Here's a little test, completely unscientific, but hopefully a bit of fun. Read the following three statements and see which one chimes with your own credo or belief and which don't, then write next to each of them whether you think the statement is Tory, socialist or Liberal:

Statement A

You cannot bring about prosperity by discouraging thrift.

You cannot strengthen the weak by weakening the strong.

You cannot help the wage earner by pulling down the wage payer.

You cannot further the brotherhood of man by encouraging class hatred.

You cannot help the poor by destroying the rich.

You cannot help men permanently by doing what they should do for themselves.

Statement B

You cannot have a just society without true equality.

You cannot demand civil responsibility from people who are excluded from the levers of power.

You cannot maintain a civil society if the gap between rich and poor is too large.

You cannot achieve social justice if the fruits of any enterprise are not distributed downwards as well as upwards.

You will never achieve the great society until the unearned privileges of the rich are removed and ordinary people's needs are placed above the selfish desires of the few.

Statement C

All of the above, but wearing sandals.

OK, which one is Tory, which one socialist and oh, alright, it's only a joke, for God's sake.

> **Quick Quote:**
>
> If you were stranded
>
> on a desert island with
>
> Adolf Hitler, Jack the
>
> Ripper and a politician
>
> and you had a gun with
>
> only two bullets, what
>
> would you do? Shoot
>
> the politician twice.

Croydon

A small Surrey suburb – or so you might think. But if you have driven through it in search of the offices of a business colleague, a friend or even an enemy, you will know that it is what scientists call a 'black hole'. Is this an exaggeration? I think not. Ponder awhile on this: I have driven through the maze of streets in Croydon for six and a quarter hours in search of an address and this is the spooky bit – I have not repeated or retraced my route even once. Every mile produced a different street or one-way system, all choked with Volvos driven by accountants in little hats.

At the end of my journey I gave up and went home. I had clocked up 872 and a half miles. So, if you are over sixty-five, don't go to Croydon. It is not a place. It is a black hole. It sucks in old people and destroys them.

PS My wife says Surbiton is worse.

Cruising

In big boats gliding through the azure waters of the Mediterranean, packed to the rim with silver-haired avuncular oldies lounging on deckchairs or sipping fine wines in the Elizabethan-themed gourmet restaurants. Smiling, white-suited stewards hovering discreetly on the immaculate decks holding trays of pink champagne, while their treasured passengers nibble on tasty snacks or doze peacefully with half-read copies of the latest John Grisham open on their laps. What bliss. Is this a vision of geriatric paradise or what? Cruising, after all, is predominantly an old person's activity, although activity might not be the most appropriate description.

A well-chosen cruise on an efficiently run ship can be, quite simply, the holiday of a lifetime for those of advanced years. For those lucky enough to have the time and the money to indulge in a round-the-world journey will find it changes their perception of life and creates a new tolerant philosophy towards foreign cultures and people of different races. Unless, of course, they happened to book onto a really naff cruise ship overstocked with clinically obese, noisy octogenarians with terminal BO, industrial strength halitosis and the propensity to fart with the resonance of a pistol shot.

On such a voyage of say 1,500 souls, eighty-three per cent will mysteriously have hailed from obscure regions of the United States, like Cleveland, or English northern towns, where the denizens have established proud reputations of 'having no airs and graces' and speaking their minds bluntly and frankly. Most of the stewards in such a cruise will be sexually deviant and the chef and his assistants will display a deep-seated grudge against mankind. The captain will be dangerously insane and subject to bouts of the Captain Bligh syndrome. A toxic virus will sweep through the ship two days into the voyage, inducing vomiting and exploding bowels of such velocity that they will register six on the Richter scale. Some people will die. Oh yes. I'm afraid so. Statistically, if you have a boatload of 1,500 mostly old people, a few are going to snuff it, even if there is no virus sweeping the vessel.

Assuming that any such virus only lasts a few days, reducing passengers to an ashen-faced gaggle of wobbling nincompoops, the next hazard to face is the first port of call in a foreign country. Here, rapacious trinket-vendors will accost the limping oldsters as they descend the gangplank to place grateful feet on terra firma.

Elderly widows from Wisconsin or the Wirral will find themselves forced to buy gross necklaces made from dried buffalo testicles or T-shirts with foreign slogans across the chest which, when later translated into English, reveal the chilling message: 'Death to Infidels' or simply 'Up Yours Bitch'.

I should state that I have never suffered any of the experiences detailed above, but I know a man who has.

I have cruised once with my wife and two friends across the Caribbean and it was an altogether splendid experience and I shall be doing it again, probably an Arctic cruise this time. It's always good to see something new:

1. Unless you love crowds, pick a smaller boat. The new luxurious, monster-sized jobs are like floating cities.

2. Go with a group of friends, if you can. A single person or an old married couple taking to the seas on a ship full of strangers can be less then ecstatic. You might end up sitting next to an accountant at dinner, who will latch on to you for the rest of the voyage and want to talk about football or double-entry bookkeeping.

3. Pick a cruise that visits places you really want to see.

4. Don't stint. Doing it on the cheap is never a good idea.

5. If your interest is in, say, ancient architecture, Islamic art or Egyptian civilisation, try to pick a cruise company that specialises and avoid those which promise 'on-board entertainment' by ageing sixtie's pop stars or 'karaoke nights'. Martin Randall is an excellent tour company for those who seek intellectual stimulation, and they do a few cruises.

6. Don't wear socks with sandals on deck.

7. Take lots of books.

8. And a pair of army binoculars.

Finally, if you do enjoy a successful cruise, be prepared for the thudding anticlimax when you get home. Suburban life in damp, old England cannot compare with the vaulting pleasure of international sea travel. This down-in-the-dumps feeling will, however, pass, especially when you start thumbing through your next Saga Holidays brochure.

So happy cruising, folks!

D

Dancing

There is little in the civilised world more toe-curlingly, mouth-puckeringly embarrassing than very old people dancing. I'm sorry to be cruel but, dammit, have you ever seen yourself – I mean really seen yourself as others – particularly the young – see you?

I might just concede that a touch of ballroom among consenting crumblies if conducted under strict medical conditions is permissible. But only in Bournemouth or Blackpool in one of those vaulted old cinemas usually occupied by bingo players. No person under the age of fifty should be admitted to witness this grotesque spectacle without a chit from a registered psychiatrist, as it has been proved to be a mental health hazard for youngsters of delicate constitution.

What is an absolute no-no, without exception, however, is grey-haired bulging geriatrics attempting to recapture a sixties dance craze such as the twist or, for the emancipated wrinklies, whose backsides have shrunk to the size of tennis balls, trying gamely to jitterbug. And if you don't know what the jitterbug is, or was, you are too young to be reading this book.

Now, those dance enthusiasts among you who are still reading, and no doubt seething with resentment, will be crying out in anguished tones that they have performed an elegant quickstep at their daughter or son's wedding or at a jolly twenty-first birthday party for a grandchild and at the end of their sweeping arabesques, the assembled company broke into spontaneous applause. Well, I say 'tish' to this. The applause was an act of relief that the participants, you, didn't actually crash onto the gleaming parquet, while seized by a massive cardiac arrest.

So, if you're old, don't dance. Oh, alright, if you must, but please, ladies, not in a floral-print dress and white slingbacks. And gentlemen, under no circumstances should you attempt to bend your partner over backwards. You are not Fred Astaire and your partner is not Ginger Rogers. The sound of a spine snapping in two is not a very happy sound. Anyway, it won't be long before 'elf 'n safety' ban dancing altogether.

Quick Quote

My heart tells me I am

21 when I dance,

Unfortunately my knees

Insist on contradicting

My heart and reminding

Me I'm 72.

Jenny Lisson

Dandruff

If you've still got hair when you're old, you'll have dandruff. Avoid plain dark clothes. Falling flakes show up on your charcoal grey suit or blue blazer.

Wear tweeds and you can shed bucketfuls of dandruff and nobody will notice. Head & Shoulders shampoo has a good reputation as a means of controlling this condition.

Death

Yes, I'm afraid old people think about death a great deal more than either the young or the middle aged. Until you are about fifty, you know for certain that dying is for other people, even if some of the other people are friends or relatives. After fifty, that certainly fades and you adopt one of two attitudes to your approaching last gasp. Resignation or foaming hysteria. If the former, you mooch about the house resolving not to buy green bananas again or rewriting your will. If the latter, you will mooch around the house resolving not to eat green bananas and tearing up your will.

In either case, you will often discuss how nice it would be if you could choose the manner of your passing. In a recent survey, Mannheim 1832, a number of ways of snuffing it were listed and people were asked to tick the one they most preferred. Can you spot the one picked by nine out of ten people in this survey, which I should confirm was conducted under strict laboratory conditions and all the interviewers were unfrocked priests:

1. Playing the harmonica in a Mongolian brothel, while dressed as Adolf Hitler – but without the moustache.

2. During an underwater trampoline contest, with a group of retired RAF dentists.

3. Quietly, in your own bed, asleep.

4. Noisily, in somebody else's bed, with five other people; two of whom weigh over 300lb.

5. Being shot dead by police marksmen while inadvertently putting the wrong kind of rubbish in your council recycling bin.

6. Being run over by a truck, packed into an ambulance, rushed to A & E, stripped down to your underpants prior to life-saving surgical intervention, only to find the surgeon wouldn't operate, because you had a hole in your sock! At your moment of death, you remember, too late, your mother's advice all those years ago.

Quick Quote:

I'm not afraid of dying.

I just don't want to be

there when it happens.

Woody Allen

Dentures

OK, so you've got false gnashers. When I was a lad, you could spot old people with false teeth a mile off and they were obviously uncomfortable to wear. A neighbour of my parents had such an ill-fitting pair that when he spoke, the top set clattered up and down as if he were sending out Morse-code signals. And he used to take them out in public and wipe them with a dirty handkerchief. Guess what? He was our local dentist.

Today, thank goodness, modern dentures are a thing of wonder, but they can still become uncomfortable. A large part of this discomfort can come from the underlying bone in the gums, which shrinks and causes an improper fit.

Adding extra calcium to your diet can slow down the bone-shrinking process as can Vitamin D. Foods rich in vitamin D include milk, salmon, tuna and sardines.

If wearing dentures doesn't appeal and you have money to burn, you can have all your gungy old teeth wrenched out and new plastic ones drilled into your jawbone. Sounds like a barrel of laughs, but not for me.

One last tip handed down to me by my father. Never lend your false teeth to another person. They never return them. Just like library books.

Dogs (Man's Best Friend)

I've never owned a dog, so I have no idea whether or not that statement is true, but many elderly people I know have dogs and they claim that a dog in the family keeps you young and gives immense pleasure. Oh yeah? Sounds great, doesn't it? Until they leap up and bite your throat out or, even worse, start humping the vicar's leg when he comes to tea.

If, however, you are a dog lover and intend to keep one until you pitch over yourself when the man with the scythe turns up, I can offer no advice. Instead, here's a few dog jokes:

- Outside of a dog, books are a man's best friend. Inside of a dog, it's too dark to read.

- Where do you find a dog with no legs? The same place you left him.

- Why do dogs rush to the door when the doorbell rings? It's hardly ever for them.

- I poured spot remover over my dog. Now he's gone.

- Noel Coward was once taking a young niece out for a walk in Hyde Park, when they came across two dogs having sex. To spare his niece's blushes, Coward explained, 'The doggie in front is blind and the one behind is pushing her all the way to St Dunstans.'

Do-it-yourself (DIY)

This is a phrase that has always driven an icicle of fear deep into my soul, largely because I have managed, over fifty-three years of marriage, to avoid performing any task, however trivial, that is better carried out by a skilled professional. Or my wife.

OK, so I'm not handy. I am clumsy. The limit of my expertise is hanging small pictures on the wall, but even this simple procedure, last attempted in 1963, reduced my family to mocking laughter, just because

I used a 6 inch screw and a hammer to complete the job. Alright already, I know I should have used a screwdriver, but they are very difficult to operate. Giving a 6 inch screw a good belt with a hammer is much more satisfactory. It's the creative artist in me, you understand.

Well, that's enough about me. How about the rest of my retired colleagues and friends? Some of you will rejoice at being asked by your spouse to carry out 'all those jobs you were too busy to complete when you were working' – or even 'now's the time to build that conservatory/lean-to/shed/garage extension or crematorium that we could never afford to have carried out by rip-off builders, who prey on old folk and rob them blind'.

If you fall into this category, I say good luck to you, roll up your sleeves and get on with it. Actually, I don't say that. I usually release a sneering laugh and say – 'Get a life, loser'. If, on the other hand, you shudder at the prospect of becoming – in your seventh decade – a cabinetmaker, an interior decorator, a plumber or a bricklayer, don't even think about starting any job, however tiny! Refuse. Firmly. Plead a bad back. Fallen arches. Dropsy. Melancholic depression. Anything. Just do not do it. It will only end in tears. Come on, you know it makes sense.

If your wife presses you, with encouraging or even threatening words, remind her of Hilaire Belloc's immortal lines, 'It is the duty of the wealthy man to give employment to the artisan', and give her a copy of the *Yellow Pages Trade Directory* QED (Quite Easily Done).

Door-to-door Salesmen

I speak with some authority here, as in the early part of my life I was a salesman. Not, however, of the door-to-door variety. This breed can be, and often are, a menace to older people.

You should adopt the following strict rules. Either:

1. Never open your door to an unannounced caller.

Or

2. Open it and state clearly and firmly that you never buy anything on the doorstep.

Quite seriously, you must. Don't fall for the patter about a student earning a few bob in his or her gap year by selling you brushes. I mean to say, is there a single household in Britain today that doesn't already own a brush? And as for that offer to tarmac your drive with what the man in the yellow flak jacket 'has left over', let us not get me started on that one, if you please.

That's about it. Just say no. Every time.

Today, however, you are more likely to be targeted on the telephone by a jaunty-sounding caller asking if you 'have thought about a new kitchen'. Frankly, I feel sorry for these sales people; after all, they are only trying to earn a living and a pretty poor one at that. Once again, just say no, politely. Don't hang on and taunt them; that's just cruel.

The silent calls are the worst and very sinister. Hang up immediately.

Downsizing

There comes the moment when you realise that your four, five or six-bedroom house with a vast garden is getting a bit much for you to manage, even with outside help. Furthermore, those spare bedrooms are probably empty for eleven months of the year, as your grandchildren rarely stay over more than a couple of times in the summer.

So you put your house on the market and gasp at how much it is now worth and you seek out a more suitable property in which to sink slowly into decrepitude. Lots of us do it. My wife and I have. Do I recommend it? Too soon to say. As I write this, we've spent less than six months in our small, new, garden-free house after thirty years in an old, rambling job, plonked in the middle of a wooded 4 acre garden. A big change. Probably the biggest change in our lifestyle we'll ever make.

You should do it, however, especially if you are prepared to be ruthless about chucking out all that extraordinary junk you've accumulated over the decades. It's a bit of a wrench, though. Even parting with that utterly pointless Tunisian birdcage that has sat in a corner of the attic for twenty-three years. Lots of furniture will have to go as well. Either to auction, grandchildren or the city tip.

The thing I found toughest to part with was books. Over the years, I had built up a library of many hundreds of books. I had bookshelves in every room, including the loo, and as the new place is half the size of the old one, it was off to the Oxfam bookshop with several carloads of my precious books.

I will confess I shed a tear when I handed them over, volumes that I had read and enjoyed over the years, but they had to go. I can only hope they eventually arrive in the hands of somebody who will get as much pleasure from them as I did.

Having downsized and adapted, more or less, to the new property, should you draw a line in the sand and say 'that's it, no more moves for us. We're only leaving here in boxes'? Well, that, folks, is a very personal decision. Most people, I guess, will say 'no more moves, it's too stressful'. Others say 'it's just a rehearsal for the final big shift of your life'. Whatever your decision, think very carefully about it; as you should when contemplating your first downsizing move, of course.

I still entertain the belief that my final move will be to a grade I Jacobean farmhouse surrounded by 16 acres of beautifully manicured lawns just off Piccadilly Circus. After all, house price collapse has to slow down sometime – doesn't it?

Dreams

I don't know about you, but the older I get, the more vivid my dreams become. I've been fortunate in as much as I can usually remember them the next morning, which most people can't. In my fifties, I used to jot down some of my more exotic dreams on a little notepad when I woke up. And before you ask; no, I never had sexy dreams. Brigitte Bardot and Marilyn Monroe didn't visit me in the wee small hours and give me a good seeing to. More's the pity.

But I did have incredibly exotic dreams, and still do. How about this: herds of elephants emerging from the spume on a palm-fringed beach, led by an army band, the conductor of which was the TV personality David Frost! Crazy or what?

Then there was the huge beer wagon drawn by four enormous carthorses thundering down a narrow cobbled alley as I stood there, pressed against a sidewall. The wagon driver was an Indian prince with a jewelled turban wielding a leather whip.

Then, of course, I still have those embarrassing dreams – and I'm sure you do, too – of being stark naked in a room full of well-dressed people. Or hunting for the loo in a gigantic office building and on finding it, being horrified to discover the toilet itself is in the middle of a vast chamber about the size of the Albert Hall.

The only really frightening dream I have had regularly is one in which the motor car I am reversing in suddenly accelerates and my frantic attempts to brake are doomed. Though, I usually wake with a start before any serious collision occurs. I reckon it's indigestion that causes this dream.

I used to peruse an old dog-eared paperback of my mother's in my early teens entitled *What Your Dreams Mean*. As far as I can recall, it contained a fair amount of pseudo-scientific claptrap, with lots of ponderous conclusions like 'this dream is clear proof that your positive impulses have been overdriven by a negative force and you should therefore repair any damaged relationships you have with your inner self'. Even at the age of thirteen, I thought this was a wagonload of tosh.

I'm sure there are modern books out there which tell you what your dreams mean, probably written by dreary, earnest, half-mad, politically correct pscyhiatrists. My wife's verdict on what my dreams mean is pretty straightforward: she thinks I'm crackers.

However, never mind what your spouse or friends say, if you have dreams, and most of us do, enjoy them. That's what dreams are for. Even try jotting down the details of the more fascinating or outrageous ones and who knows, you might have the basis of a fantastic novel or a new Bond film. On the other hand, you might just be crackers.

Some people claim they can predict or even choreograph their own dreams. They insist it's simply a matter of willpower. Just concentrate, Zen-style, on you're wished-for dream and hey presto, you'll fall asleep that night and enjoy a performance that would put Busby Berkeley to shame. An old army chum of mine Peter Higton says he often forces himself to have a dream where four beautiful women glide into his bedroom and entertain him. My guess is that this is usually after he's consumed a bottle of Famous Grouse and a tumbler of vintage port.

I've not tried it myself, the forced dream. With my luck, the four ladies who come gliding into my bedroom would be: Patricia Hewitt (ex-health minister), The Bride of Frankenstein (name your own), Dawn Primarolo (current health minister) and dear old Polly Toynbee (Guardian columnist).

Drink (Alcohol)

Hardly a day goes by without some government minister, dome-headed scientist, rabid social worker or a researcher from one of the 16,412 Alcoholic Concern organisations that now exist, in Islington alone, warning us that we are doomed, because of our love affair with booze.

They may be right. I have no idea. And what is more, I couldn't give a toss about what they think. I am seventy-four. I would also assume that if you are reading this book, with or without artificial aids, you are yourself over sixty. Therefore, we will not concern ourselves with the social problems of binge drinking or vomiting in our city centres. This is an exclusively young person's activity.

Neither will we come over all guilt-ridden about the booze-filled chaos that follows and sometimes precedes football matches on a scale that makes the sack of Carthage in 146 BC positively benign. Football hooligans, it will be conceded, may count among their number a few old people, but so few as to make it statistically irrelevant.

What we are talking about here is old people enjoying a few drinks after lunch, dinner or whenever – as they have done for the best part of their adult life. Having enjoyed over the years enough Claret to float a small flotilla without ever being drunk, I resent being told by some twerp with a clipboard and a degree in 'Nit-picking Studies' that more than one large glass of wine a day is bad for me. It isn't. Neither are two.

Wine is a very civilising thing. It has warmed the body and spirit of countless numbers of people over the centuries from paupers and popes to beggars and barons. We old people know what's good for us – and how much is bad for us – and it varies from person to person.

So, the next time some health fascist starts banging on about middle-class drinking at home being a 'problem', do what I do, uncork another bottle of Chateau Lynch-Bages and raise two fingers of your free hand in a slow, meaningful gesture. You will then experience a glow of satisfaction that some people claim is not unlike the receiving of extreme unction by a priest. Frocked or unfrocked, according to taste.

Quick Quote:

I feel sorry for

people who don't

drink. When they

wake up in the

morning, that's as

good as they are

going to feel all day.

Dean Martin

Driving

Avoid wearing silly hats while driving. It will encourage road rage as you weave along in the centre of the road in your 11-year-old saloon and cause the young stud behind, with a shaved head and a nose ring, to hurl abuse at you.

Never wear those driving gloves with little holes in the back. Only prats wear them. OK. So you're an old prat? Fine. Don't blame me if your grandchildren mock you and never refer to fast drivers by saying 'Who does he think he is – Stirling Moss?' Your grandchildren will never have heard of him. You might as well say 'Who does he think he is – Attila the Hun?' That'll really fox them.

Quick Quote:

Youth would be infinitely

more enjoyable if it came

in middle age.

Bill Brown

Dry Skin

Many of us ancient wrinklies will have skin that over the years has weathered and aged like old parchment and those of us who have spent time in their youth under the sun, lounging by the side of Mediterranean swimming pools or on tropical beaches, will, at worst, have an epidermis not unlike the hide of a Nile crocodile or, at best, a newborn Galapagos turtle.

So what the heck? It's too late, isn't it? There's surely nothing we can do about it? Well, yes there is. We can stop the clock. Stop it, not turn it back.

If you are a touch leathery and you want to halt the progression and avoid ending up with your face resembling an old cavalry saddle, here are the six vital steps to achieve this noble objective:

1. Stop using soap. Hot water is all you need to keep clean. But rub yourself vigorously with a loofah or coarse-grained flannel.

2. After bathing, use moisturiser liberally. My mother swore by Ponds Cold Cream and she had a lovely complexion at the age of eighty-three.

3. Don't sunbathe. Strictly verboten. And use a sun block – factor twenty-five minimum.

4. Drink lots of water – at least eight pints a day (see 'B' for Bowels) – and cut down on your hard liquor intake.

5. On retiring to bed, moisturise your face and hands like crazy. Good, plain moisturising cream is cheap, so spoil yourself and don't forget behind the ears.

6. Write the above down on a Post-it note, stick it on the fridge and do it all!

E

Ears

Old men grow hair in their ears – great tufts of the stuff. Remove it or turn it artfully into little ponytails. Be careful if you buy one of those battery-driven hair-removal devices, because a sudden tremor of the hand could drive the pencil-like implement into your brain, which could prove somewhat disagreeable.

Old ladies should avoid heavy earrings, because the ancient ear lobe is not noted for its load-bearing qualities. A distant aunt of mine once sported a pair of huge brass bangles and her ear lobes slowly stretched, until they reached her elbows. Well, almost.

Ear Trumpets

Not unless you are auditioning for a part in a Victorian melodrama or engaging in sexual congress with a deaf hooker.

Ear Wax

OK – it's a distasteful subject, but oldsters do produce quite a lot of it. Try storing it in a small jar; it can come in handy for blocking draughts from small keyholes. Never rummage in your ear hole with a match, especially if it's lit.

Erections (Male)

For the elderly, they still occur – from time to time – but usually at the wrong time. I mean, who needs a hard-on when travelling to Hackney Wick – alone – on the top of a number fourteen bus?

Avoid Viagra and other artificial aids. If your brewer's droop is permanent, then that's just what nature intended. Oh, alright, a couple of Viagra is permissible if you are on an 'old boys' reunion' in Amsterdam. But never in Macclesfield. They have no use for such fripperies up north.

The late Jeffrey Bernard, who wrote a column entitled 'Low Life' for *The Spectator* magazine, once claimed he was so surprised on waking with an erection in his latter years that he took a photograph of it. I believe it was briefly considered as a runner-up for the Turner Prize.

PS Ladies, please, if you get an erection, a phone call to the *Daily Sport* or even Max Clifford may be the first step on the way to a fortune.

Exercise (also see 'J' for Jogging)

No, I'm not going to suggest you throw away your Zimmer frame or snap your favourite walking stick over your knee. Neither am I going to suggest you enrol at the local gym and spend six hours a week on one of those treadmills or leg-press machines. What I am going to suggest – nay positively implore you to do – is some form of physical activity every day that increases your heartbeat a little and gets those old lungs pumping oxygen, provided first – and this is important – you ask your doctor if it is OK for you to do so.

The best possible exercise for old people is, in fact, walking. A brisk walk every day can work wonders. But what if you can't walk? Or can only limp along with the aid of that stick? Then, you can exercise while sitting down. You can swing your arms, you can extend your legs from a seated position or you can ask your doctor or that nice boy who runs the gym for some simple sedentary exercises that will achieve – albeit gently – those two crucial things: deep, full lung breathing and an increase in your heart rate.

Let me emphasise again: you must exercise only after you have discussed it with your doctor. But medical opinion generally will agree that maintaining physical activity in old age is more conducive to longevity than slumping in an armchair and allowing everything to seize up like an abandoned motor car.

It is an established fact that taking in copious amounts of oxygen through exercise is a splendid way to quickly increase your energy. However, if you are unable to walk unaided and even gentle movement is difficult, then deep breathing is an excellent substitute. And I mean deep. Inhale slowly, while counting as you go. Exhale slowly, taking twice as long as inhalation to count. This exercise alone done regularly will energise the body by increasing oxygen levels.

So, off you go and if it's only breathing exercises you want to perform, you won't have to change into a singlet, shorts, jockstrap and sweatband, either.

Experts

Of the kinds who proliferate on television to add authority and weight to whatever fatuous, newfangled nostrum is being peddled by politicians or government spokesmen. It has long been a golden rule of mine to disbelieve any pronouncement made by a so-called 'expert'. This is not to say they (the experts) are always wrong. But, by the same token, they are not infallible.

For example, the BBC (God Bless Auntie) is fond of wheeling in some swivel-eyed expert to comment on, for example, the conflict in Iraq or Afghanistan. No, the individual is not a soldier or even an ex-soldier with front-line experience; the individual is an 'expert'. This strange breed, often with a domed forehead and appalling dress sense, is described in *Cassell's Dictionary* thus: Dexterous from use and experience, practised, skilful, a scientific or professional witness.

Ask yourself how many of these 'experts' you observe on television fulfil that definition. Particularly that bit about being a 'professional witness'.

So, be sceptical, try to gauge a second opinion, if you can, before you act on some apocalyptic pronouncement made by an 'expert' and remember, Nostradamus didn't get everything right in his predictions. Except when he did.

Confused? Exactly. That's what 'experts' want you to be; it enhances the mystique of their calling and keeps you in a state of perpetual apprehension.

Quick Quote:

Abortion is advocated

only by politicians

who have themselves

been born.

Ronald Reagan

F

Fashion

It is impossible for old people to be trendy, so don't even go there. One of the most stomach-churning, buttock-clenching, tooth-grinding sights is a septuagenarian in jeans and trainers or a baseball cap; although, nobody of any age should ever wear one unless, of course, they are the President of the United States or the Dalai Lama.

Filling Time

When you retire, one of the things you will have in abundance is time – twenty-four hours of it, stretching like a vast desert beyond the horizon, gaping, awesome, even frightening. And this huge wilderness is waiting, silently, to be filled. An old friend, now deceased, once said to me that the time spread out before him when he first retired was like some monstrous, invisible beast that had to be fed with a diet of activity every day forever. To ignore the monster's hunger pangs would condemn him to a slow, downwards slide into decrepitude.

Of course, unlike my friend, many retired people find it easy to fill their declining years with a whole raft of activities and the monster is replete, well fed and tranquil. Not for them the nightmare question of 'what do I intend to do with the rest of my life?' Such people, and I am one, do find the pressure to fill their time by taking up some new activity very hard, indeed.

After a life crammed with incident, travel, other people, noise, excitement and challenge, to be urged on retirement by well-meaning friends and relatives to take up a 'hobby' can strike icy terror in the heart. The word 'hobby', perhaps one of the most depressing in the English language, conjured up to me visions of basket weaving, morris dancing, making cathedrals out of matches, birdwatching, ferret strangling and bowls, most of which, I will confess, are adopted enthusiastically by many thousands of retired people, not just willingly, but with genuine delight.

The challenge, therefore, if you are of my admittedly difficult and selfish disposition, is to find a way that feeds the monster of time without actually seeming to do so. This may sound a trifle oblique, so let me put it another way. If you are engaged in an activity so absorbing that you find time flies and there are few, if any, moments when you sit slumped in armchair gazing helplessly into the future, then you have found the Holy Grail, the gold at the bottom of the rainbow, and the monster will remain satiated for the rest of your life.

Under no circumstances, however, should you allow yourself to be bullied into taking up some weird and grotesque hobby just to 'fill in time'. It won't work and the monster will regurgitate it and spit it back in your face. Find, if you can, that which truly enriches the soul, nourishes the mind and challenges the body. Easily said – damned difficult to locate.

The happiest retirees, in my opinion, are those who can carry the interest and activities they enjoyed while working seamlessly into retirement. For these lucky people, there is no need to dabble in the unknown or to force themselves into fake enthusiasm for yodelling, yoga or yapping (a style of bookbinding in leather with flaps at the edges). They just carry on as before, but more so!

Food

Whatever food you eat, whether a rare steak, a vegetarian pie or a bowl of nourishing porridge, you will spill some down your front. Regularly.

A man I know, who shall remain nameless, has spilled so much stuff over his regimental tie that once a month his wife boils it up to produce a nutritious soup; that's real recycling.

So don't be ashamed of tucking in a napkin at mealtimes.

Footwear

Apart from Dr Scholl's fine selection, there isn't a lot to choose from. Best to avoid open-toed sandals though; yellow toenails like broken parrot's beaks or corns the size of pickled onions are not aesthetically pleasing. Cover up is the best rule.

Old people should avoid laces, too; they require a certain amount of bending to do them up. The same goes for socks. There are, however, devices on the market rather like a pair of tongs, with which you grip the sock and then, while standing upright, (but resting your body against the wall or door) you simply drag the sock onto the foot. Without the necessity of bending over. I've never used one of these devices personally; although, one day soon, who knows? You can buy them on eBay, but not at Harrods. Or, alternatively, dispense with socks altogether and have your feet tattooed dark blue.

Quick Quote:

I've got the immaculate

feet of a 21-year-old. I

keep them in the deep

freeze.

Don White

Fossils

For those of us who have in recent years been described as 'fossils', even by the occasional loved one, it's worth knowing just what the word means.

A fossil is the petrified remains of a prehistoric creature that has been excavated by somebody wearing cleated boots, khaki shorts and a pith helmet. But the actual word dates from the sixteenth century and comes from the Latin *fodere*, 'to dig'. It was originally used to describe a fossilised fish that had been dug up by somebody in tights and a ruff. Yes, a fish.

So when the next person calls you a fossil, you know what he really means is you are a silly old fish head. I'm sure you feel better for knowing that.

Quick Quote:

The best thing to

do is to behave

in a way befitting

one's age. If you

are sixteen or under,

try not to go bald.

Woody Allen

G

Gas

The sort produced from the human stomach and expelled through orifices. Never apologise. Let rip and enjoy it, except if sharing an intimate moment in a telephone kiosk.

Gas (Manufactured)

Always remember to turn it off before you go on holiday or go all electric.

Glamorous Grannies

Whenever I hear some septuagenarian being described as a 'glamorous granny', my stomach heaves and the hairs on the nape of my neck spring up erect.

Then my worst fears are confirmed, when a photograph of the old lady thus described appears in the newspaper or some glossy magazine. There, in all her pristine horror, sits a creature whose looks owe little or nothing to Mother Nature but rather speak a slavish devotion to the surgeon's knife, the Botox injector and the wig maker. Not to mention the attentions of some crazed dentist with a surgery on Harley Street.

But if you look hard enough, you will see through the artifice and the clever photographic retouching and reality will emerge. This is an old lady who is trying to emulate somebody thirty years younger: the hairstyle, the cleavage and the bee-stung lips.

And there are giveaways that even a good photographer may miss. Like the hands. OK, so the false nails in shocking pink look oh so up to the minute, but what about those knuckles and the hint of arthritis in the fingers?

Alright, enough already. So I like grannies to look like grannies. Is that what I'm saying? Well, sort of. But looking your age doesn't mean wearing a mob-cap and black taffeta. What it does mean, though, is dressing and grooming oneself with a degree of dignity. Grannies can look serene and beautiful without making complete prats of themselves and poncing themselves up like Madonna (no, not *that* Madonna, Grandad – the pop star Madonna, who once wore ice-cream cones over her breasts).

The cult of youth may yet end in tears as more and more old people try to emulate the younger generation. The same applies to old men, who still think they are James Bond and wear tight jeans and shirts open to the navel.

Let's face it, glamour is for the young. It is superficial, tenuous and eventually fades. Don't try to be a glamorous granny or grandad – be yourself, because real beauty comes from within.

Quick Quote:

Once accused of being lazy,

President Reagan said,

'I know hard work never

killed anybody, but at my

age I thought, why take

a chance?'

Glasses (Spectacles)

If you yearn to look wise, try the half-moon glasses worn on the end of your nose. Always buy six pairs Make that ten pairs – oh, what the hell, twenty! – at a time and leave them in various rooms about the house. I don't need to tell you why. Any good chemists do a very good pair of reading specs for fifteen quid!

Global Warming

The first thing you need to know about global warming is that it is *your* fault (see 'E' for experts). The scientific community – whatever that is – have stated that not only is planet earth warming up, but it is the fault of us humans. Apparently, we are leaving carbon footprints all over the place with an air of casual disdain. So, what exactly is a carbon footprint? And why a footprint! In the old days, the London bobby investigating a burglary would say, 'This job has got Sid the Safe-cracker's *finger* prints all over it.'

Even for allowing that the scientific community have got it half-right, we shouldn't panic. There is nothing the scientific community and the government, of whatever complexion, like more than scaring the pants off us at every opportunity.

Stay calm, don't cancel your holiday or sell your car and take up cycling, things are not as bad as the doom-mongers would have us believe. Just modify your consumption. Yes, just modify it. Don't be panicked into the sort of cringing, politically correct huddle that politicians would love us all to adopt.

What's that? You think I exaggerate? Well, think again. In an increasingly affluent and complicated society, where the political class are regarded with contempt (particularly by older people, who see them for what they really are – self-serving control freaks), politicians of all stripes and hues are very worried by the apparent indifference we, the public, have about their claims to be 'there to serve us'.

OK, so what has this to do with global warming, you may ask? Simply this, dear reader. By exaggerating the problems of global warming and getting us to swallow every nuance uttered by the scientific anoraks and government pundits, we are then more than likely to accept their lust to control our lives and regulate our behaviour down to the smallest detail.

Yes, I know the ice caps are melting. But do you honestly think that by forgoing that holiday in Tenerife and getting July frostbite in Frinton you will make a halfpenny of difference? Come on, get real.

Look, we've had an ice age and lots of other periods where most of the earth's surface became tropically hot. Swings and roundabouts. And who is to say we won't get another ice age in a few thousand years from now.

Sadly I, and I imagine you, won't be around in fifty years time to see the gloomy prognostications of the 'we are all doomed, unless we give up smoking, eating red meat, having sex, driving cars, flying to the Med and actually enjoying ourselves' brigade proved to be not only wrong, but to have been talking complete bollocks for years.

Here endeth the lesson.

God

Does he exist? Do you believe in Him? Is there anything up there, apart from limitless space? Just what is religion for? Are you a devout churchgoer, a supporter of some established faith, or are you, like most older people, a sort of casual, half-believing agnostic?

Maybe you are none of these things and are a declared atheist, a fervent admirer of the Richard Dawkins' school of thought in *The God Delusion*. Whatever you are, or are not, remember this: we old folk are a lot closer to finding out whether God exists than most people.

I was brought up as a fairly unenthusiastic Christian, hardly ever visiting church unless it was for weddings or funerals. I never really thought much about whether God was a delusion or that religion, as Marx so neatly put it, was the opium of the masses.

But as I get older, I begin to ponder more deeply about the great questions of our time. The meaning and the point of life itself, why we are put on this earth in the first place and so on. Now I am in my seventies, let me state quite unequivocally that I do believe in God and I do believe that the fundamental tenets of Christianity are the basis of living a good life. Of course, I've fallen short on many occasions, but I do know that there are such things as right and wrong and good and evil.

Clever atheists like Richard Dawkins demolish the idea of God and kick holes in the ritual of prayer, because they cannot scientifically prove that God exists. Big deal. You cannot scientifically prove that He doesn't, either. Faith cannot be dissected by scientific analysis and God, who is beyond science, is not to be found in a laboratory.

To those scientific materialists, whose fundamental hostility to religious belief is as fanatic as any foaming Islamic extremist, I say: 'you will not find science able to explain why you fall in love, why you are moved to tears by music, why a sense of patriotism rises in your heart or why, when you gaze up at the heavens on a clear day, you find it impossible to grasp, in human terms, how space goes on forever'.

I write this as daffodils are bursting out in a yellow and gold profusion and swans glide past on the river, all miracles of nature or, as I believe, of God.

So, folks, don't give a second thought to Dawkins and his ilk. They've missed the point. Faith, by definition, cannot be proved to be either true or false.

And lastly, if God does not exist then, in the words of that splendid Michael Caine movie of the sixties, What's It All About, Alfie?

Quick Quote:

God was here, but He

left early.

Comment by a priest surveying the
killing fields of Vietnam

Golf

Now, golf – a game associated in my mind very much with old-age pensioners – is one I have never played. It has remained a great mystery to me as to why people on the verge of retirement often smile smugly when asked what they are going to do and say, 'Improve my handicap.' When I was a child, hearing this expression led me to believe that the handicap they proposed to improve was perhaps lameness, deafness, incontinence or trapped wind.

But no. It was all about knocking a little ball about over open fields in fancy dress and at tooth-loosening expense. So my advice to you golfing oldies, don't try to improve your handicap, sod that for a game of soldiers, have fun instead. Chuck away your number three iron and use a dead swan (make sure it's been in the deep freeze overnight. Oh, yes, and make sure that it's dead). Grip the swan by its body and, using the long, willowy, frozen neck, swing its head against the ball with every ounce of strength you can muster. This is guaranteed to get you talked about in the clubhouse.

Second tip: cheat. Why not? You've cheated the grim reaper thus far, so what's the big deal about cheating to win against that pompous prick who is always boasting that he's played nine holes with Tiger Woods in a charity match and had him worried. And don't be shy about harassing your opponent as he is about to drive off the first tee. Farting with the resonance of a pistol shot just as he hits the top arch of his swing is, I am told, invariably successful. Bribing his caddie to grease his clubs with goose fat is another winner.

But enough about golf. You will have sensed that I am a teensy weensy bit biased against the game.

Quick Quote:

Playing golf is like

going to a strip club.

After 18 holes, you're

tired and most of

your balls are missing.

Tim Allen

Gout

Something of a joke condition, except to those unfortunates who suffer from it. We have all seen cartoons or old silent movies, where some poor old duffer, usually a red-faced, retired colonel, has got his gigantically swollen foot swathed in bandages and propped up on a stool.

Gout is a very painful complaint; a form of arthritis than can be inherited. It is caused by a metabolic malfunction of proteins that creates high levels of uric acid in the system. The acid forms crystals, which lodge in the joints, often the big toe (ha-ha!). Hilarious isn't it?

Men are the most likely victims of gout; women rarely suffer from it. Strange to tell, but cherries may help to alleviate the symptoms of gout, either tinned, frozen or fresh. Don't ask me why or how.

I wonder where that saying 'life's just a bowl of cherries' came from? Probably some bucolic colonel in Budleigh Salterton with his foot in a turban.

Grandchildren

Almost everything anyone writes about grandchildren will be drenched in cliché, moist with sentimentality and dripping with panegyric whitewash. Or is it just me?

OK. Let's accept right away that the three grandchildren I have been blessed with are perfect in every particular. Having got that off my chest, let's have a short, sharp dose of reality, shall we?

If you have grandchildren you are very likely to be enjoying them just as much as you enjoyed your own children, possibly even more so. You may well have been seduced by the cosy images created by writers of fiction about the joys of grandparenthood.

White-haired and avuncular, you sit in a wing chair by the side of a roaring fire, while your grandchildren, their innocent faces scrubbed and gleaming, listen to your dispensation of knowledge and wise counsel. They gasp respectfully as you regale them with gaudily embellished tales of your life and times. You are the repository of all knowledge and your wisdom spills out gently into their eager, waiting ears and they, about to embark on life's journey replenished with your genes and your blood, will carry forward the torch passed to them, which was passed to you by generations past and still burns brightly today, with a fierce and ethereal light.

G

Hold on, what was it I said about clichés? Oh, alright, let's skip that bit and move on.

These days, grandchildren, mine certainly, are supremely self-confident and cynical; wise, even, beyond their years. My youngest grandchild at the time of writing is thirteen, computer literate, fashion conscious, opinionated and more aware of life's vagaries and sorrows than I was at the age of seventeen.

We have to realise that they consider their own parents (i.e. your children) as being a bit old fashioned and out of touch. And as for granny and grandad, well, work it out for yourself. But they remain a delight, a promise of adventure, a sense of continuity.

Their childhood passes in a flash, they become young adults almost overnight, too soon, much too soon, most of us oldies agree, but that is the reality. The horrible, inevitable consequence of a society that is racing towards a dangerous, noisy, uncertain future.

So listen to your grandchildren – you may learn as much as they learn from you. Be patient, as I am not, to my shame. Cherish them and if, by good fortune, you become great-grandparents, rejoice that you may be twice blessed and enjoy all the pleasure and pain again for the second time.

Graveyards

OK, let's face it, you'll be visiting a few funerals before you 'parttake in your own' and although they can scarcely be described as fun occasions, you will have to accept that they are part of the great cycle of human existence. There is also an etiquette to be observed at graveyards and one which should be taken extremely seriously.

For example, if kneeling at a graveside, don't turn to the person next to you if he or she is older than you and say, 'Do you think it's worth going home?' And don't do any of the following at a funeral, *please*:

1. Goose the widow as she bends to throw dirt on the coffin

2. Take mobile phone calls at the graveside

3. Toss handfuls of rice onto an open coffin and shout 'maggots'

4. Drive behind the hearse and keep sounding your horn

5. Turn up at the chapel of rest dressed as Adolf Hitler

Finally, remember that after the ceremony at the graveside, people should then celebrate the life of the deceased. It's what he or she would have wanted. Isn't it?

Quick Quote:

It is depressing to think

that there may be no life

after death. Particularly

for those who have

bothered to shave and

brush their teeth.

Anon

Grumbling

Let us get one thing absolutely clear. Grumbling is an exclusively male phenomenon. Grumpy old men grumble, women don't – it's as simple as that.

Don't be fooled by those excruciatingly unfunny television programmes in which second-rate female comediennes twitter and sigh about their lot in life. They are not grumbling. Really, they are *not* grumbling. What they are doing is what old women do instead of grumbling. They are moaning (see 'M' for Moaning).

Back to the grumpy old men – we cantankerous old has-beens and never weres. It is, after all, our duty to grumble. It is expected of us and so we mustn't disappoint. Just what you grumble about is a matter of personal choice, but do try to be a bit original and add a touch of variety to your grumbles.

It's pretty pathetic to confine your grumbles, for example, to the weather, politics, your bad back or the state of English football. Try grumbling about failed rice crops in Cambodia or the flaws in the theory of relativity. Be creative, for God's sake, you miserable old duffer.

And while you're at it, try working out why grumpy old men grumble. Why don't they 'grumple'? Grumble has a 'b' and grumpy has a 'p'. Nobody has ever explained that to me and it makes me very grumpy.

H

Hair (Male)

If you still have any, keep it short. Unless you are one of those lucky ones with a head of luxuriant white curls like Father Christmas. Mostly, however, long-haired old men look very dodgy, especially if they hang around on street corners in grubby mackintoshes. And never do a comb over, leave that to footballers, Donald Trump and certain TV presenters.

If you've lost the lot and your dome resembles a boiled egg, you can give endless pleasure to your grandchildren by inviting them to draw pictures on it with felt pens. Or, in extreme cases, when the doodling of grandchildren becomes a bore, nip off to your local tattooist and have a map of Southern Tibet – or West Clandon, the choice is yours –tattooed tastefully across your skull.

> ### Quick Quote
>
> I'm not bald. I'm
>
> just taller than
>
> my hair.
>
> Clive James

Headaches

We've all suffered from these to a greater or lesser degree. About ninety per cent of all headaches can be classified as 'muscle contraction' or, more commonly, as 'tension headaches'.

Some unfortunate people are born with a biological make-up that means they are headache prone. For, I guess, the majority, who have occasional 'headache days', here are a few tips for those of us who fall into this category:

1. At the start of a headache, take a couple of Aspirin. (Not lots, two would be sufficient.)

2. Do some light exercise. It releases stress.

3. Deep breathing, really deep, can help. Do it for five minutes.

4. Self-massage can also be helpful. As can acupressure. The two key points for reducing pain with acupressure are the web between the forefinger and thumb and under the bony ridges of the back of the neck. Use both thumbs to apply pressure there.

5. Put a pencil between your teeth, but don't bite. No I'm not crazy. Try it. Just hold it there for five minutes and think nice thoughts, or even nice dirty thoughts. It works for me.

6. Go easy on salt.

7. Don't skip regular meals.

8. Laugh.

But, dear reader, don't try to do all the above at the same time. You'll put a crick in your back.

> **Quick Quote:**
>
> For my sister's
>
> 60th birthday, I
>
> sent her a singing
>
> mammogram.
>
> Steve Wright

Health & Safety Executive

Old people should decide for themselves that the health & safety executive is either:

- A benign arm of the government dedicated to the well-being of its citizens, monitoring safety at work and at home and ensuring that the multifarious risks that punctuate our daily lives are minimised by the dedicated and selfless civil servants who work tirelessly on our behalf.

Or

- A bunch of Nazi control freaks who, with copies of *The Guardian* or *Das Kapital* stuffed in the back pockets of their jeans, seek to expunge from all middle-class life any hint of pleasure or the smallest possibility of any risk, however small.

At the time of writing, the health & safety executive has 398,000 employees, all with gold-plated pensions and free Hush Puppies provided by the taxpayer. Male employees get a beard allowance of five grand a year. Actually, so do the women. (Alright, I made that up, but it sure as hell seems like 398,000.)

If you have played conkers since the age of six and are partial to hanging baskets and walking along railway lines – preferably with a glass of Scotch in one hand and a fag hanging out of the corner of your mouth – in the nude, ignore the blandishments of the 'Elf & Safety' busybodies, who think these activities are dangerous, and carry on to your heart's content.

Hearing Aids

A blessing or a curse? Of course, the modern hearing aid, perfected by clever scientists with German-sounding names and bulging foreheads, are a huge boon for the deaf.

Did you get that? The deaf. Not hard of hearing, or the audibly challenged. D.E.A.F.

So, if you are suffering from a touch of the old Mutt and Jeff, there are several splendid devices on the market, which can alleviate your symptoms. But even the most sophisticated of hearing aids can turn nasty and give you a shock. Not of the electrical kind necessarily, but more of the social variety.

A dear friend of mine, now deceased – sorry, dead – was a keen theatregoer and one evening, during a particularly poignant moment during the performance of Sheridan's *School for Scandal*, his admittedly rather antique hearing aid began to emit a high-pitched electronic shriek. An old lady on his left suffered from a touch of the vapours and the leading actor on stage, in mid peroration, went cross-eyed and fumbled his lines.

Fortunately, the theatre manager, a man known for his nervous disposition, was prevented from phoning for the fire brigade, as he was tripped up on his way from the auditorium to his office by a ginger-haired accountant from Penge, who was fleeing from what he thought was a terrorist outrage.

Lessons were learnt. My old friend said that it was his fault for fiddling with the volume control.

He also said that on one occasion, travelling to London on the train, he was unfortunate enough to be seated next to a cretinous oaf in a pin-striped suit, who was bellowing fatuities into his mobile phone. Most of the other passengers in the carriage were cringing behind their newspapers, being British and trying to ignore it. My friend just switched off his hearing aid and completed the journey in blissful silence.

This is when a stupendous truth dawned on him. Unlike ordinary people with perfect hearing, he could choose what he listened to and what he didn't listen to.

I thought, wow, how wonderful. All we need now is for those Nazi clever Dicks at the national thingamajig to come up with a selective hearing aid that can blot things out; for example, all that extraneous and hideous background music that the BBC will keep playing over the dialogue in a play on television.

Or, even more splendid, the ability to blot out politicians' replies to John Humphrys' questions on the *Today* programme, many of which are in the *Guinness Book of Records* and are not only long but incomprehensible. One I believe, aimed at that sexually incontinent, fat fellow who played croquet and drove two smart motor cars, lasted a full seven hours, fifteen minutes and thirty point four seconds. Or so it seemed. The question, however long, was infinitely more interesting than the waffling garbage that passed for an answer.

With the new, special, super-selective Third Reich hearing device, which is soon to be invented, you could blot out forever sounds that offended your delicate ear.

And don't forget to tell your grandchildren that listening to loud pop music and frequenting night clubs that specialise in hellish amplified sound will, in the long run, ruin their hearing. That's not just the opinion of an old grumpy; medical opinion is universally agreed that excessive music sound will damage young people's ears.

Quick Quote:

Queen Elizabeth is

a lady whom time

has surprised.

Sir Walter Raleigh prior to the queen's death in 1603.

Hernia

Not exclusively an old person's ailment, but it does occur with monotonous regularity among the elderly. There are two common types of hernia and they are both more likely to hit men than women. Hiatus hernia causes part of the stomach to bulge into the chest cavity.

The chest cavity? Afraid so, Grandad. It happens. The nasty thing about a hiatus hernia is that there are rarely any symptoms apart from a back-flow of stomach acid into the oesophagus, which can cause heartburn.

The inguinal hernia is more common and it occurs when abdominal tissue bulges through a weak spot in the abdominal wall in the groin area. It's no fun. I've had it. But it's easily fixed if you go to your doctor as soon as you feel that tender swelling in the groin. The operation today is a relatively simple repair job.

To avoid getting a hernia is really a matter of common sense. So, no heavy lifting, lose weight, avoid constipation, heavy coughing and sneezing and no more knee-trembling sex up against a wall with that 16 stone barmaid from The Cock and Ferret.

Hip Replacement

Old people seem to dominate the list of patients awaiting hip-replacement surgery and in Britain alone, many thousands of oldies have had their lives immeasurably improved by this procedure. Some folk have had both hips done at the same time, anticipating wisely that number two hip is likely to go shortly after number one gives up the ghost. I have even heard of a man who had both his hips replaced, even though they were operating quite smoothly. He was, however, eighty-three and an American. 'Why wait for the pain to kick in?' he explained. 'Go for a refit while you're still mobile.'

It's not so strange when you think about it. Some young women have a 'mastectomy' performed on a perfectly healthy breast if their family history on their mother's side shows a history of cancer, having been told by their doctors that they have inherited the faulty genes that lead to this awful disease.

Back to the hips for a moment. Men – you can avoid this prospect of surgery if you have kept your hips gently active throughout your youth and, more importantly, your middle years. If you are still mobile and wish to maintain healthy hips, try the following exercise every morning for the rest of your life. No, really, don't tut-tut. Read on and trust me, I'm not a doctor.

Stand upright with your hands on your hips, feet apart at the 'at ease' position. Now, raise your right leg laterally and as far as it will go without discomfort. Even 6 inches or so initially will do. Repeat fifteen times, but slowly. Change legs and do the same with the left leg.

Do this every day without fail. The whole procedure will take less than three minutes. After a week or so, increase the repetitions to twenty-five for each leg. Do it slowly. Don't jerk your leg upwards. Make it glide and then fall naturally. It doesn't matter if you can't get your legs up to be completely parallel to your waist, for that's almost impossible, but what is possible and, indeed, desirable is a constant flowing movement, so that your hip joints are being given a proper workout. But, I repeat, do it gently and slowly.

OK? Want to try it now? Better wait until tomorrow morning before breakfast preferably. In America, they do it to music, but we Brits don't have to. I find Radio 4 quite sufficient.

History

A subject that younger people seem less and less interested in. But, to grow up without a sense of, or even slight knowledge of, history is little short of tragic. Older people have a better understanding of the distant past, mainly because they have lived through it and even those whose education was no more than rudimentary were taught the basic details of history by teachers who were not infected with the plague of political correctness or who preached the doctrine of moral equivalence.

Perhaps it is too late to turn the clock back (it usually is) and expect youngsters to have a profound knowledge of the past. They should, however, acquire a broad understanding of their own history, the history of Britain. Not by remembering lists of dates – Waterloo 1815, Indian Mutiny 1857–1859, First World War 1914–1918 – but by appreciating the really incredible achievements of this small island race.

H

We older folk have a duty (yes, yet another one) to pass on to the next generation some salient facts about British history. First of all, remind them what a remarkable bunch their ancestors were and how Britain led the world in so many fields. Tell them how Britain was a world leader in the nineteenth century and was, in fact, the founder of industrialisation.

In the eighteenth century at the height of our powers, we produced two thirds of the world's coal, five sevenths of its steel and we spun over half of its cotton cloth. Tell them the British were key players in the development of the steam engine, the telegraph, electric light, pneumatic tyres, radar, telephone, television, the fax machine, the jet engine, computers, penicillin and much more, which you can look up at the British Library when you next have a day trip to London.

Ask them who invented football and cricket and then, as they gasp in surprise, tell them how the British developed vaccination, mains sewerage and antibiotics. Tell them not to believe all this modern revisionist guff about the British Empire being all bad. It wasn't. It was a mixture, and what a mixture! At its peak, the British Empire covered a quarter of the earth's surface, it introduced many positive benefits to the people it ruled and, to be truthful, it obtained lavish benefits itself which, after all, was what imperialism was more or less about.

It did all this with a tiny army and a handful of dedicated civil servants and administrators, who set up systems of government, law, communications and, of course, in many countries, the English language, which is now accepted as the primary language of the business world.

Tell them how the evolution of such things as habeas corpus and trial by jury were influenced by Britain. Tell them of the signing of the Magna Carta by King John at Runnymede in 1215, which sowed the seeds of our enduring and enviable constitutional monarchy. Tell them that the Duke of Wellington, who defeated Napoleon at Waterloo and prevented Europe from being dominated by the French emperor, was the greatest general in the history of the planet. Tell them that the British Navy dominated the world's oceans for over 100 years, owning over half of the world's warships, and that it paved the way for the spread of trade and early commercial globalisation. Tell them that Lord Horatio Nelson, who defeated the French again at Trafalgar, was the greatest admiral of his time.

Tell them all this and more if you can and hope, or even pray, that they may remember even a quarter of it.

Holidays

Saga holidays are the best. No question. But you should mix in at least one other vacation where there are younger people, too. If you choose a holiday which promises an activity programme, make sure you don't sign up for any of the following:

- Projectile vomiting
- Underwater motor cycling
- Morris dancing
- Necrophilia (unless accompanied by a tasteful string quartet)

On holidays, know your limits. If your legs are a touch wobbly, don't visit the Himalayas. Always nap in the afternoons. Take a bucket of high-factor sun lotion with you, even in Iceland. Never believe that couple from Budleigh Salterton who say, 'You must come and visit us at our little cottage in Devon.' Old men should not flirt with the waitresses. Nothing is sadder than an old bloke whose mind is making promises his body can't keep. Old women should, however, allow themselves to be rogered senseless by Spanish waiters. It's all part of entering into the spirit of local customs.

> **Quick Quote:**
>
> The devil himself had
>
> probably re-designed
>
> hell in the light of
>
> information he had
>
> gained from observing
>
> airport layouts.
>
> Anthony Price

I

India

If you can, visit India. Apart from being a beautiful country with breathtaking scenery and exotic architecture, you will find most Indians speak better English than most British natives at home. Sure, we grumble about call centres in Delhi, but for my part, listening to the exquisitely modulated tones of an Indian lady telling me that my call is important to them and to just hang on is as pleasant to the ear as the late John Geilgud reciting Shakespeare.

> **Quick Quote:**
>
> Travel broadens
>
> the mind, but sitting
>
> at home just reading
>
> the brochures,
>
> broadens the bum.
>
> K. Leeming

Infidelity (Old People Having It Off With Anybody Other Than Their Partner)

It happens. Not a lot, I'm sure. But there are rules to be observed. It's all about sexual etiquette. Here's a few tips:

Things an old man shouldn't say to his equally ancient mistress during sex:

1. I can see right up your nose

2. Muriel used to do that

3. Is it in yet?

4. It's good being in bed with a lady I don't have to inflate

5. Sorry. It must be the baked beans

Things an old lady shouldn't say, even to her twenty-year-old lover during sex:

1. I want a baby

2. Do you smell something burning?

3. Do you know your ceiling needs painting?

4. Does it come up with an air pump?

5. You probably thing I'm a terrible flirt

So, folks, even if you're tempted, don't do it. Except in your dreams.

Quick Quote:

I went to a restaurant

that serves 'breakfast

any time', so I ordered

French toast during

the Renaissance.

Steve Wright

Ink

You know, the stuff that used to come in bottles. You can still buy it, if you are willing to search the more expensive shops in the West End of London or, failing that, Reykjavik in Iceland. The ink alone, however, is not enough. You will need a pen with a nib. A nib! How often have you heard that word in the last twenty years? So, fully equipped with your little bottle of Watermans, if they still exist, and with your pen with a nib, write that letter you've been meaning to send to the local council complaining about drains, rubbish collection, local paedophiles, CCTV cameras or whatever. Always sign off with the phrase 'Yours faithfully, a concerned citizen'.

Remember to blot it, with blotting paper – do they make the stuff any more? – and send it off by Royal Mail to your local council. Always use a first-class stamp. One thing, and one thing only, I will guarantee is that you will get a prompt reply. You see, council jobsworths are so sick and tired of receiving semi-literate emails, dodgy faxes and impertinent text messages that a lovely letter, hand written, in ink, on a really nice piece of creamy notepaper, will be treated with awe and respect.

Will the council do anything about your complaint? Give me a break. This is the twenty-first century. Nobody gives a stuff about some whingeing crumbly, who thinks everything's going to hell in a handcart. All I promised was a reply to your letter. That would be nice, wouldn't it? What did you expect, a round of applause?

Quick Quote:

On my school report once

was a comment by the teacher

I couldn't read. When I asked

him to tell me what it said,

he replied irritably, 'It says –

write legibly.'

Gray Jolliffe

Insurance Companies

As an older person, your views about insurance companies will fall, more or less, into one of three broad categories:

1. You are grateful for the sense of security they give you with your house, life, motor car and holidays, all happily insured.

2. You are comfortable in the knowledge that you, your loved ones and your various bits and pieces are covered, but you find the steep increase in premiums a bit hard to swallow.

3. You believe, with some solid justification, that insurance companies are thieving, conniving, dishonest, crafty, bureaucratic, bloated, profiteering swine, who will refer you to the small print in the

event of you making even the most derisory claim. After studying clause 73B, subsection 98, you are made aware that the whole purpose of insurance is to enrich the insurance company and for them to find evermore devious and complex ways of robbing you blind and never paying up – ever.

Which of the three categories do you fall into? OK, maybe category three overstated the case, but not a lot, I venture to suggest.

Here are some simple guidelines for retired people who are reviewing their insurance arrangements, as all newly retired people should:

a) Always get alternative quotes for your house, car and holiday insurance. Remember, you are the customer. You can and should drive a hard bargain.

b) Always offer to pay an 'excess', i.e. say the first £1,000 of any private medical claim or £500 on any motor-car claim. This will reduce your premium substantially.

c) Never insure with a company that shoots you the line that 'older people' are a greater risk for car and holiday insurance. Tell them to go and get comprehensively stuffed.

d) When insuring your house, its contents or maybe a second holiday home, tell them of your history of claims on say your motor car; if you've insured your various cars for say twenty-five years without a claim – tell them. It means you are a good risk.

e) Cast a very beady eye over your private health insurance, if you have any. Today, more than ever, insurance companies are reluctant to cover you in the event of long-term illness or care without hugely expensive premiums. You must make a judgement whether or not it's really worth that monthly premium of £200, £300 or more for private medical care. Or, alternatively, would you be better off tucking the equivalent of the premium into an interest bearing savings account?

If you are reasonably healthy and use the good old National Health Service for minor aches and pains, just consider this imaginary scenario: a 65-year-old couple who live to be eighty-five and who make no claims on their private health insurance will have donated say £30,000 in premiums to their insurers, with nothing, save peace of mind, to show for it. If, on the other hand, they had put the same amount into a savings account, they would have accumulated £30,000 plus interest. That's one hat-full of cash, folks. Bugger peace of mind.

Invisibility

Becoming invisible, the extraordinary phenomenon that happens regularly to old people when they are waiting to be served in a shop, is a most irritating condition. Only last week, my wife, who is seventy-six ,was standing at the till of a local shop, while behind it were three female sales assistants, all wearing uniforms and badges on their lapels that revealed their names: Stella, Sharon and Ribena (although I could be mistaken about the last one).

The tallest of the three, almost certainly a Sharon, was engaged in a lurid conservation with the other two about the events of the previous evening at a local club. Altogether too much detail was being disgorged, most of it of a neo-pornographic character. The other two, Stella and Ribena (or was it Rubella?) were listening, agog, while occasionally glancing at their fingernails, whose prehensile protrusions were clearly not entirely natural. My wife, who is admittedly only 4 foot 11 inches, tried in vain to attract the attention of the three by smiling, coughing, saying 'excuse me' and holding up her shopping basket.

Now, and here's the sinister thing, my wife is used to becoming invisible, but at the precise moment she actually disappeared from view, the three girls behind the counter became stone deaf. Coincidence or what? Spooky isn't it?

There is a method by which old people, especially old people under 5 foot tall, can prevent themselves from becoming invisible. Unfortunately, most old people in general, and my wife in particular, refuse to adopt my fail-safe method on the grounds that it is bad-mannered and two wrongs don't make a right.

However, here is my fail-safe method for preventing invisibility in shops, supermarkets, cinema queues or restaurants and I hope some of you at least may find it useful when you feel yourself fading into the ether like dissipating smoke:

1. Approach the counter or till at a brisk trot (or a brisk hobble if you've got a touch of arthritis)

2. Adopt a wild facial expression

3. Release a high-pitched keening sound (think wounded panther or buffalo on heat)

4. Announce in clear tones that as you are a sufferer from acute diarrhoea unless you are served immediately, a severe laundry malfunction will take place

Trust me on this one; it really works, even on a girl called 'Ribena'. Sorry, GlaxoSmithKline, Ribena is a nice blackcurrant drink full of vitamin C. Actually, it's a nice name for a girl, too.

J

Jogging

A ludicrous activity at any age, but among the elderly, positively insane.

There has been an increase in the number of over sixties taking to the road of late, their spidery legs poking out of baggy running shorts, their thinning hair plastered over their sweating domes and bony chests covered with vests decorated with absurd slogans like: My other body has been loaned to Arnold Swarzenegger'.

OK. They think they are doing themselves some good. Surely they are? But wait. Jogging on hard pavements or tarmac roads throws a tremendous strain on the joints and half-naked geriatrics create visual pollution as they totter by. Motorists cannot be blamed if they reach out of their car windows as they pass an ancient jogger and jerk his pants down.

So, if you're over sixty, don't jog. Walk instead. Briskly. And properly attired. It really is better for you, Grandad, believe me, I know.

Joints

Those on our elbows, knees, hips and elsewhere will definitely become dodgy over time. Gentle exercise will keep them operational, more or less, but remaining sedentary will only hasten the inevitable. Joints tend to make cracking noises, like pistol shots, if you move suddenly. I know an old man who can crack his knuckle joints to the tune of *Rule Britannia*. If you want to earn the admiration of younger people, try practising the knuckle, knee or elbow crack to the latest hit by Take That. Avoid traditional hymns if possible and don't opt for the Rolling Stones; they're probably older than you. Incidentally, the reason the Stones play so loudly in concerts is to mask the sound of Jagger's hips going off like firecrackers.

Finally, a serious tip. Take fish oil tablets daily; 324 should do the trick and keep those joints working like Rolls-Royce pistons.

Joints (Smoking)

Take up puffing the odd joint only if you have been a non-smoker all your life and you are over eighty-two. Why not?

Quick Quote:

A gentleman always

takes his weight on

his elbows, even at

the risk of carpet

burns.

Peter Cadbury

K

Kipling (Rudyard)

If you've never read a book of poetry in your life, or even if you have and hated it, now you're seated in life's waiting room by the door marked 'exit', go out quickly and buy the complete works of Rudyard Kipling.

There are two poems in it that you must read, even though you totter at the very rim of senility. Not only must you read them, and reread them, you must learn them by heart, line for line, word for word. Then, at Christmas time or other family celebrations, you can recite them to your grandchildren. They are perhaps the two most moving, life-enhancing poems ever written in the English language. They are: *Gunga Din* and *If.*

Of course, you should read the rest, too, but these two are the jewels in Kipling's crown. If you can't find them when you totter off to your local bookseller, then get your son, daughter or grandchildren to seek a copy out on the Internet. Not to acquire a copy before you push up the daisies will condemn you to an afterlife in fiery hell. OK – have you got my drift?

> **Quick Quote:**
>
> Bloody clever that
>
> Kipling bloke.
>
> Wrote all that poetry
>
> and still found time
>
> to make excellent
>
> cakes.
>
> A Pub Drunk, 1987

Kissing

There is only one important rule old people should know about kissing. Grandchildren do not like being kissed on the lips by drooling old nitwits. And taking your teeth out before you plant a smacker on those rosebud lips only makes matters worse. I remember an aunt of mine, now long deceased, who used to hit you full in the face like a plunger unblocking a sink. On a number of occasions, I thought I was going to drown in saliva (hers) or suffocate.

So when greeting a young person, kiss on the cheek only. OK? And keep your mouth closed.

> **Quick Quote:**
>
> I'd rather have my
>
> sinuses drained than
>
> actually kiss a
>
> punter on the lips.
>
> A Las Vegas Hooker

L

Lavatories

I'm sorry to have to keep lowering the tone but, frankly, old people do have a special relationship with the loo. To start with, they need to use it a lot more than younger people. For those unfortunates among us who need to visit the loo say fifteen times a day or more, here are some tips:

If you are off to town for some shopping, collecting your old-age pension or taking your prescription to the chemist, make a clear plan of your route in advance, writing down on your small, pocket-sized, local map all the places where a quick widdle can take place. Most department stores and cafes have facilities, but their being called 'restrooms' is further proof of the Americanisation of Britain. Public toilets are, on the whole, best avoided. They are often tatty and unpleasant and they have notices pinned up inviting you to put a pound coin in a little slot in return for three brightly coloured condoms, whatever they are. If all public loos were as pristine and inviting as those in Royal Windsor, it would be a pleasure to pop in, do the necessary and admire the splendid wall tiles that depict moments of British history. But watch you don't splash your shoes.

Having noted where all the free loo facilities are in your town, you should plan your route, if walking, so that you are seldom, if ever, more than three minutes from any one of them. This is not as difficult as it sounds and what is more, you will acquire a useful knowledge of local geography.

When visiting friends, try to make sure that you have 'been' before you set out. Young people are a bit touchy about crotchety old men, in particular, who lock themselves in their beautiful designer bathrooms for half an hour and use up all their candy pink striped loo paper and break the flush handle by excessive use.

It is an established scientific fact that people over sixty-five need to flush three times per visit. Every year after sixty-five, the number of flushes required increases by the following ratio:

66 years of age	6 flushes per visit
70 years of age	8 flushes per visit
90 years of age	0 flushes (the incidence of chronic constipation in 90-year-olds makes flushing

Watch out for telltale signs of disapproval when visiting young friends or relatives. If, as you announce your intentions to 'visit the bathroom', they immediately send a pet canary ahead of you to enter the loo after you have finished, you could be dropped off their invitation list for the future. And even if you are invited back, you can be sure as hell they won't serve you asparagus for lunch again.

Quick Quote:

Regret no solids.

Notice in Indian Public Lavatory

Liposuction

Even the word is enough to make your toes curl and your gums recede – liposuction. This is a medical/cosmetic procedure, whereby a nurse in a starched uniform sticks a pointy thing attached to a hosepipe into your stomach and in another room an enormous retired all-in wrestler, with biceps like a sprinter's thighs, operates a foot pump that sucks all the yellow, slimy fat out of your midriff and squirts it into a bucket.

Then you go home with baggy skin hanging like an apron from your navel to your knees, having signed over a cheque for £3,249.75 to cover the costs of the procedure.

For old, fat people who can't be bothered to diet or exercise, is this really an option? I think not. I know they say it's a 'safe' operation, but I remain sceptical. Just suppose the man operating the 'sucky-pump' goes bananas and goes on sucking after all the yellow sludge has been drained out and sloshed into the bucket? He could hoover out your kidneys and your liver, and maybe even a lung. Not a very pleasant prospect. So, fellow oldies, don't even think about it!

M

Manna (as in manna from heaven)

Originally, manna was food miraculously supplied to the Israelites in the wilderness. A sort of divine food with supernatural properties. Old people often have their own version of manna. A favourite treat, perhaps, usually food, and often something quite simple. Try this simple test: you are on a desert island, alone, and you can have just one luxury food item to supplement your diet of worms, beetles, coconuts and bananas. Mine is Marmite. A 4 gallon vat of the stuff would see me through until that rescue ship steamed into sight on the horizon. What's yours?

The Master Race

Not, as you might assume at first glance, a reference to Nazi Germany in the forties, a period most people over sixty-five will have lived through. The master race I allude to is perhaps better described as a 'tribe'. The members of this tribe are not joined by blood ties or even ties of a social class. They can be white, black, yellow, male or female. They operate, however, not unlike a master race. Who are these people?

They are our political class. Politicians of all persuasions make up this group. The most vivid description of them has been provided by the brilliant political journalist Peter Oborne. In his seminal book *The Triumph of the Political Class*, he exposes the new-style political animals, who now occupy both sides of the House of Commons and, to a lesser extent, the House of Lords. Oborne argues that the old tradition of duty and integrity, which blossomed in the nineteenth century, has been corrupted by venality, nepotism and mendacity. The new ruling elite in Britain are motivated by professional self-interest, protection and advancement, rather than old-fashioned ideology.

The exclusive club that is Westminster looks after its own like a modern Mafia. Gold-plated pensions (paid for by us), lavish expenses and a cross-party conspiracy to exclude us, the voters, wherever possible. They are, in the literal sense of the word, professional politicians. Many of them in all three major parties have never held real jobs in the real world. They are creatures of an opaque and exclusive fraternity. It is terrifying to observe that a man or woman, whose only experience of running an enterprise of any size has been as a student union leader and a political research assistant, can nevertheless be appointed to run a vast organisation like the Health Service or the Home Office. When they fail, as they often do, they are simply moved to another post and we, the mugs that we are, have to shoulder the consequences. The differences between the main parties in Parliament are now so slight, wafer thin, in fact, that a visitor from Mars would be unable to distinguish any real difference whatsoever.

So what, if anything, can we older, wiser people do? Not a great deal, I'm afraid. The rot is setting in and I believe it threatens the very fabric of our democracy. Do, however, when voting, try to judge the personal quality of the man or woman who is canvassing for your vote. Don't let any of the parties fob you off with a tame party hack and ask for your cross on the ballot paper just because he or she wears the party rosette. Don't be afraid to vote against the party you usually support if the candidate on offer is, in your opinion, unlikely to represent your interests vigorously in Parliament.

Much the same applies to local politicians and local elections although, at local level, you are more likely to find a genuine candidate, who really wishes to serve their constituents faithfully. Finally, if you are really concerned about the behaviour or performance of your Member of Parliament, make a fuss, become a nuisance, write to the papers, phone the party headquarters, make your voice heard. Aren't you fed up with being part of the silent majority?

Masturbation

Alright already. I'm not going to bang on about the subject for too long, so you can wipe that frown of disapproval from your face and try to listen.

Masturbation: even the word gets your nose wrinkling in disgust, doesn't it? Well, it shouldn't. Masturbation is as old as life itself and it might have been invented just for old people. Anyway, the majority of us, whether male or female, have at some time enjoyed this solitary vice. Except it isn't a vice. It's a release. Never mind that our mothers or teachers warned us that it would make us go blind or grow whiskers in the palms of our hands. It's perfectly natural and for old people who find they can no longer perform the gymnastics of conventional sex, or are bereft of a sexual partner through death, divorce or decrepitude, the big 'M' is a boon.

Let's end on a lighter note and, you will be relieved to know, I am not going to mention the various nicknames for the big 'M', save for just one: The Five Fingered Widow.

There, that wasn't too bad, was it? Lighter note? Oh, yes, here's a list of reasons why old people in particular should embrace the joys of the big 'M':

1. It's free

2. You meet a better class of person and one who is unlikely to criticise your performance

3. You won't have to buy a candlelit dinner as a prelude to seduction

4. It's harmless fun

5. It can be performed while wearing headphones and listening to Mozart

Media

We now live in a media world, or global village, and much of what we know and think is shaped by the media. The great debate, if it exists at all, is not between the people and their political leaders, but a kind of jousting tournament between the media and the politicians.

Even in the days before television and the Internet, newspaper barons were once described as 'harlots, exercising power without responsibility'. Today, the ownership of media corporations crosses national boundaries and much of our own media is in the hands of foreigners.

In the thirties, the Canadian Lord Beaverbrook owned *The Daily Express*, then a hugely popular and powerful daily paper. He went on to become a minister in Churchill's war cabinet. Later, we had Roy Thomson, also a Canadian. Then the staggeringly powerful Rupert Murdoch, an Australian, and, more recently, Lord Black, another Canadian, although he has fallen from grace.

It won't be long before a TV network or newspaper group will be owned by a Chinese or Russian tycoon. You think I'm kidding? Think again. Media outlets concentrated in so few hands do, I submit, present a danger to democracy. While individual editors and journalists are mostly fair and objective, they are still just hired hands and if their bosses have a particular axe to grind, it is hard for them to resist. And today's editors of national papers are extravagantly well paid; £600,000 a year is not uncommon.

For old people in particular, an attitude of healthy scepticism towards all media is absolutely essential. This said, I must confess that the modern media are also, paradoxically, great guardians of democracy. Yes, as well as a threat (I said it was a paradox). Think of the great crusading campaigns of recent years, like the exposure of the thalidomide scandal and the appalling cases of child abuse.

Many newspapers, including the tabloids, have done magnificent work in their investigative campaigns, as has my old medium, television; BBC at its best and Granada's *World in Action*, to name just two examples.

But old people should still remain sceptical. We should watch both ITN and BBC news. We should read at least two daily papers, preferably with opposing views. Only by doing this will we be able to reach our own informed and balanced opinion. I know. I worked in the world of media for over thirty years. And, in this country, at least we still have a free press, in spite of all my reservations.

So, enjoy your viewing and your reading and make it as diverse as possible – provided you take it with a pinch of salt.

Quick Quote:

On each of my birthdays,

I mourn the flight of one

year of my youth into

nothingness, the growing

blight upon my summer.

Tempus Inreparabile Fugit

Oscar Wilde

Memory Loss

We older people all suffer from it to a greater or lesser degree. At its worst, of course, it can be the early stages of Alzheimer's. A study conducted at The National Institute of Mental Health showed that a substance called lecithin can improve memory in normal, healthy people. Lecithin is available in health shops, but I would ask your doctor before embarking on a course of the stuff.

Diet can help, including a regular intake of folic acid, iron, calcium, magnesium, zinc, copper and vitamins C, B1, B2, B3, B5, B6 and B12. When I first heard this, I assumed you could only take your meals in a chemistry lab, but you can get the benefits if your diet includes milk, bread, cereal, lean meat, poultry, seafood, fruit and vegetables. Oh, and eggs. They apparently contain lecithin, choline, zinc and all the 'B' vitamins.

Well, you can take that advice or ignore it, but most people's diets do include most of the above anyway. Personally, I believe a mid-afternoon snack can boost your memory and concentration. A bit of chocolate is my preferred choice. Oh, alright then, a big bit of chocolate.

There was something else I was going to tell you, but I've forgotten what it was ...

PS I've just remembered. Apparently, standing on your head and letting the blood rush to your brain will help the memory cells. However, I don't think it is such a good idea for the over sixties. Ask your doctor before you try it.

Mirrors

A tricky one this. Looking at your own reflection in a mirror can come as something of a shock to old people. And quite suddenly, too.

For over fifty-five years now I had looked at my face in a mirror while I shaved, until one day, without warning, I saw my father staring back at me. I thought it must a trick of the light, because my dad was old, nearly seventy. Then I realised that's what I was, plus some. How come I had reached Dad's age so quickly? It didn't seem quite fair.

If you have mirrors around the house, go for the smoked glass variety, they soften your image and those wrinkles like the Grand Canyon on your cheeks and neck seem to disappear. Never have full-length mirrors in your bathroom. The reflection of a naked, steaming octogenarian rising from the foam is like seeing a re-run of *The Creature from The Black Lagoon*, or Bela Lugosi in *The Wolf Man* (RKO pictures, 1931).

Moaning

Moaning is what old women do instead of grumbling (see 'G' for Grumbling). Old women do like a good moan. It clears the head and it flushes toxins out of the system.

There is an art to moaning and in the hands of a skilled operative, it can reach heights of Himalayan extravagance. But there are rules. Old women can only moan about situations or things that are male orientated or which have been caused or influenced by men. The actual moan, when uttered, must also be at a time and a place where there is no possibility of any solution, cure or alleviation of the thing being moaned about.

For example, you are on holiday in Tenerife, one late afternoon, and you are sipping a splendid cocktail with a chunk of fruit stuck to the rim of your glass. Your wife looks up at you from her sunbed and says, 'The fridge door at home still won't shut properly. I thought you'd fixed it. When we get back, the kitchen will be full of ice.'

This is a classic female moan. You are thousands of miles from home and some domestic fault, usually a result of your own incompetence, is brought up at cocktail hour, when you are just reflecting on how splendid life is.

Don't worry, though, the female moan is just part of life's rich pageant and we old men must bear it with a patient shrug as, in the words of Shylock in Shakespeare's *Merchant of Venice*, 'Patience is the badge of all our tribe.'

Mobile Phones

OK, let's cut to the chase. Mobile telephones are the most useless, pointless, socially divisive bits of stuff that have ever been invented. People have been bullied, cajoled and shamed into owning the damn things. Teenagers in inner-city areas stab each other and steal them. Businessmen in striped suits bellow down them on trains. Schoolgirls with brains no bigger than a walnut gabble inarticulate rubbish into them as soon as they leave their school premises. Salesmen with silly haircuts and their jackets draped over the seat of their Mondeos yap into them, while trying to hold their cars steady at 85 miles an hour with one hand. Heavy users fry their brains like pork sausages and their skulls eventually explode in a cloud of blood, pus and tissue. Old people, above all, should avoid them like the plague.

Why in heaven's name would you want to be 'in touch' with anybody when you are sauntering down to collect your pension at the post office? If you've survived sixty plus years without one of the cursed instruments, do not start now. Be honest, have you ever heard anybody having an intelligent or even crucial conversation on a mobile phone? And do you want bigger, taller, uglier mobile phone masts springing up all over your neighbourhood, sending out toxic waves that will cause dogs to give birth to three-headed puppies and vulnerable old ladies to suddenly grow nipples between their shoulder blades?

What's that? You *do*. Very well then, we'll just have to agree to disagree and don't write to me in a year's time after you've acquired a mobile phone and complain that you've gone deaf and lame and your forehead is covered in cauliflower-like protrusions that squirt poisonous sludge all over your M&S cardigan. You have been warned.

Music

Music, it is said, can soothe the savage breast. Recent research in California has revealed that, for the elderly, music, carefully chosen, can orchestrate their moods to an extraordinary degree ('The effect of music on the elderly', 1998. Karl Fresh Institute, Los Angeles, California).

Even if you are not a music lover at all or if your taste is high classical, pop or jazz, music can be as great a mind-altering agent as the ingestion of chemicals. To summarise the findings of the admittedly obscure Karl Fresh Institute, they found that in old folk's homes, for example, the best music first thing in the morning, while old people were waking, was soft, orchestral strings or recordings of birdsong. Then, after they were actually up and staggering about their ablutions, some racy jazz acted as an uplifting stimulus. By mid morning, swing and big band music replaced jazz and by mid afternoon, choirs and female singers would fill the air with gentle ballads. At bedtime, not surprisingly, the type of music which had the right soporific effect was, again, soft orchestral.

It would be interesting to see if this package of background noise would work on a group of English old folk. It might smack of canned elevator music and this would not have a very calming or stimulating effect on the listener, instead inducing extreme irritation. It was not clear whether the Californian experiment allowed the participants to disengage or switch off at any time. If the music was piped in, I imagine you had to take it neat or invest in earplugs.

It also occurred to me that a person at the old folk" home with a mischievous sense of fun might switch the tapes around and sit back to see the effect of Wagner's *Valkyries* at full volume played at 6.00 a.m. while the oldies were snoozing. Or the regimental march of the Grenadier Guards blasting ancient eardrums just as the dear old souls were climbing into their winceyette pyjamas in readiness for beddy-byes.

Quick Quote:

I have everything I

had 20 years ago,

except now it's all

lower.

Gypsy Rose Lee

N

National Health Service (I)

This extraordinary and uniquely British institution is rarely out of the news these days. Politicians of all stripes and colours claim to be staunch defenders of it and it certainly absorbs eye-watering amounts of money from us, the taxpayers, while being one of the biggest employers in the country.

Now, we old people have, or should have, a special relationship with the NHS. The vast majority of us will need to use it in our declining years and many of us will die while in an NHS hospice or care home. For some elderly people, particularly those who live alone, the prospect of surrendering ourselves to the care of the NHS can produce worries and anxieties. We are constantly bombarded with statistics by the government telling us which hospitals have reached which targets and which hospitals haven't. The quality of care varies from one NHS trust to another, which only adds to our worries.

But, for most of us, the tales of malpractice, dirty wards, dodgy surgeons and other scare stories are often anecdotal. The popular press loves scaring the pants off us from time to time and it's hard to separate whether what is reported is genuine fact or politically biased exaggeration, either left or right.

The NHS should not be a political football. It should be above the rough and tumble of debate 'twixt Tories, Labour, Liberals and the rest.

OK. So you are an old person and you can still get about unaided. You visit your local GP for the odd ache and pain and you swallow whatever pills and potions they prescribe. Maybe you've never been inside your local hospital yet. Believe me, lots of old people haven't. Not even the A & E department. You are curious about just what does go on in the wards, so you might visit a sick friend or relative, but this only gives you a snapshot of what goes on, not a fully rounded picture.

Well, here's what I did. I became a volunteer at my local hospital. Just a few hours a week – and it was an extraordinary experience. I could see at first-hand how nurses and staff react under pressure. I could discreetly observe how clean the loos and the wards were and how the patients were getting on. (I helped in the geriatric ward.)

Now, two things emerged from this experience. First of all, I realised that most hospitals in the NHS would be in serious trouble were it not for the hundreds of volunteers who supplement the full-time staff. Secondly, most volunteers, not all by any means, but a fairly large majority were older people.

Keeping an eye on what might be your own future is a most rewarding experience, a bonus if you like, on top of the genuine sense of satisfaction you get from being a volunteer. So, if you are still mobile and not carrying any unpleasant viruses like bubonic plague or jungle fever, why not volunteer at your local NHS hospital? You will gain so much from doing so, believe me, and what is more, you will be an extra pair of eyes to spot the odd malfunction (dirty loo, remains of a ham sandwich dropped on the floor behind a bed).

However, let me make it clear. You must not become a snoop. You just do the job given to you by the hospital and simply observe while you perform your tasks. It's easier for a volunteer to point out some simple problem than a paid employee, who might be apprehensive about building a reputation as a disloyal whistle-blower.

Finally, let me repeat, you must not become a snoop, just a volunteer who observes and, in observing the myriad details of life in a busy hospital, you will also find that giving of your time is perhaps the most rewarding experience of your life. By being part of the NHS, you may be able to influence its future. Not much, perhaps, but every little helps.

PS I have learned, from careful observation, that successful use of a bedpan is more difficult and, indeed, dangerous than traversing the Grand Canyon blindfolded on a tightrope, while wearing soccer boots, a crinoline and balancing a live parrot on your head.

National Health Service (II)

OK, the NHS is such an important issue for old people that it deserves two parts. So, to paraphrase Max Bygraves – 'I wanna tell you a story'. And for those of you who don't know who Max Bygraves is, you are too young to be reading this book. Buzz off to the disco or some other hell-hole that caters for the 'yoof' culture. Oldies may read on. Thank you.

Well, it's not so much a story that I want to share with you, but a dream. A very strange dream. A very strange dream, indeed. The day prior to my very strange dream, I had read a report in the newspapers that hinted, with subtle menace, that heavy drinkers and obese people might be refused treatment at NHS hospitals on the grounds that they were 'self-abusers'. I think smokers were mentioned, too.

Anyway, that evening, after a meal of stunning opulence washed down by a bottle of claret, I enjoyed a large Cohiba cigar and a balloon of fine cognac before retiring to bed. The dream – or possibly nightmare – that followed went something like this: a government announcement was transmitted on national television, read by a ghastly harridan, who was billed as Gauleiter of Health or some such title. In short, it clearly stated that in future, the NHS would deny *all* treatments to people who:

1. Smoked

2. Were fat

3. Played dangerous sports

4. Went on holiday to dodgy parts of the world

5. Drank more than a thimbleful of sherry once a fortnight

The policy, this harridan maintained, would ease the burdens placed upon the NHS by selfish, drunken fatties who stank of fags, played anything more vigorous than dominoes and holidayed any where outside the UK.

Within weeks, waiting lists had disappeared and most wards in hospitals had a few empty beds. The government claimed a vital success and decided to move the policy a notch further. This time, they declared that people with sexually transmitted diseases, drug addicts and old folk who had minor car accidents, would also be refused treatment. Within a month, the NHS was running like a Swiss watch and surgeons were on a three-day week, with no reduction in pay.

Building on this brilliant policy, the government then pushed it to its ultimate limit. The NHS would not treat anybody who was injured, sick, drunk or crazy, because these entire ailments were self-inflicted. A couple of months later (my dream was moving at a cracking pace), it was now clear that the NHS would not, ever again, treat sick people. They were just a drag on the workings of the National Health Service. It was a zero tolerance policy.

Not too long after this draconian decision was implemented, a few hospitals reported that they had received no admissions, no patients and not even a stray drunk lurching into A & E. 'Brilliant,' declared the health harridan.

However, after a further month or so, a number of hospital managers became worried that the nursing staff were sitting around in empty wards playing cards and surgeons were out on the golf course four days out of seven. On the other three days, they were hanging around car showrooms eyeing Lamborghinis and Ferraris with lascivious intent. It got worse. Cleaning staff at hospitals demanded a rise in pay to compensate for the boredom they suffered by having no work to do.

Then, an imaginative chief executive at a large NHS hospital decided that as the government would not let them treat sick people – any sick people – they would have to treat healthy people, instead. Teams of junior doctors roamed the streets asking perfectly fit and healthy people if they would care to accompany them to the hospital for a 'routine check up'. Most people refused. A sense of desperation ensued. Some NHS trusts did manage to collar a half-dozen or so citizens for check-ups. Other trusts were unable to pull in anybody at all.

Desperation was replaced by a sense of rivalry. Hospital managements realised that if they didn't treat anybody, they might lose funding, so they set up snatch squads to pull people off the street and whisk them over to A & E. A rash of kidnapping broke out and innocent, healthy citizens began to avoid going out at night for fear of being whisked off to hospital and checked over by avaricious medical students.

Questions were asked in Parliament, but the government claimed that their NHS policy was working well, albeit with a few teething troubles

One particular NHS Trust, near Slough in Buckinghamshire, was anxious to win favour with the government, so they instituted a cunning plan. They had done quite well so far in treating robustly healthy people. Their method was to hide well-built male nurses behind hedges or fences and then have them leap out and chloroform their victims, before driving them off to hospital in unmarked hospital vans. The chief executive of this particular trust (near Slough) announced his cunning plan to a packed hospital management conference at a secret location (also near Slough).

In future, one in three of the healthy victims they snatched in the street would actually have a minor operation performed on them. Soon, other trusts followed suit. Minor operations became major operations. Healthy football players had kidneys removed for no good reason. A famous tennis player who was not pregnant received an abortion. An elderly nun from Ipswich had four toes amputated. Competition between hospital trusts raged. Soon, robust members of the public were having pacemakers fitted, heart transplants and brain surgery.

The policy ended when a particularly zealous surgeon in Birmingham operated on a middle-aged man and amputated all four of his limbs. As the wretched fellow lay recovering from surgery, a crazed dentist broke in to the hospital, kidnapped the patient, whisked him off to a nearby dental facility and pulled out all of his teeth. The man, it was later revealed, was a local MP and junior minister at the Ministry of Health.

Shortly after this, I woke up – palpitating – and resolved to cut down on the brandy before bedtime.

Naturism

That people choose to become naturists and prance about naked in this country has always remained one of life's mysteries to me. Even more astonishing is that so many of them seem to be old people, too.

You've seen those little magazines they publish with photographs of happy couples playing ping-pong or queuing up at the barbecue. I would have thought frying sausages in the open air with lots of naked people about was a highly dangerous business. Occasionally, there is a news item on television featuring nudists. They seem impervious to the fact that all their bits are heading south and wearing sandals when you are naked looks plain ridiculous.

If you are old and you must become a naturist, go abroad and do it there. Preferably in a hot country. And no photographs, please; not even if you are playing ping-pong.

Quick Quote:

This Government is

useless, pointless and

without function –

like men's nipples.'

Gerald Nabarro MP

Necrophilia

A most disagreeable thing, necrophilia. But as Groucho Marx probably didn't say: 'You'll never know if you're a victim of Necrophilia, which is something of a blessing in disguise'.

Quick Quote:

My grandfather

is very forgetful,

but he likes to

give me advice.

Last week he took

me aside and left

me there.

Nostalgia

Yes, I know, nostalgia is not what it was, but it is something that afflicts old people alone, because young people have nothing to be nostalgic about. When reminiscing or engaging in nostalgia (see 'A' for Anecdotes), old people tend to exaggerate and review their past through sunshine-tinted lens. This is fine, indeed obligatory, but there are a few things we should establish before we gush sentimental claptrap in front of an audience of young people.

There wasn't really a 'golden age' when we were young: a time of hot English summers, virgin milkmaids gambolling through fields of daisies and all the other picture-postcard nonsense we like to think defined the twenties and thirties. It was a time that blew hot and cold, that was at times wonderful and at other times simply dreadful. Just like today, in fact. So let's knock a few specific myths about our past on the head, shall we?

These are somewhat personal and you may disagree. If you do, I couldn't give a toss. I'm writing this book, not you:

1. Laurel and Hardy were never funny.

2. Neighbours didn't just drop in to borrow a cup of sugar.

3. Trains didn't always run on time.

4. Al Jolson, a Jewish man who blacked up and pretended to be a Negro soul singer, was a pretentious arsehole and a rotten vocalist.

5. Vera Lynn wasn't a forces sex symbol. (I mean, she never posed in her knickers, did she?)

6. The quality of acting in the early days of television drama was not just bad, it was excremental. I am convinced, as an ex-TV man myself, that the BBC has a secret training programme for actors called 'The BBC school of shouting'.

7. Women's fashion in the forties wasn't 'classic', it was high frump.

8. London's streets may have had less litter than today, but were ankle-deep in dog poo.

9. Politicians weren't all models of propriety and completely free of sleaze. We just never found out.

10. Marilyn Monroe and Elizabeth Taylor only had nice figures from the waist up. Both had big hips and rotten legs.

11. Most public building from the forties on was shoddy, utilitarian and ugly. A number of famous architects, who have been ennobled by pusillanimous governments for their 'cutting edge' designs, really deserve to be put up against a wall and set fire to as a punishment for inflicting things like The National Theatre and The Barbican on a supine public.

12. Food in most English restaurants, including the top hotels, fifty years ago was just a notch above pig swill. Oh, alright, two notches.

So, armed with these truths, or others that suit your own prejudices, you can now reminisce nostalgically, secure in the knowledge that the young people on whom you inflict these recollections will:

a. not believe a word of what you're saying, and

b. tell the same version of these past lives when they reach the outer rim of their old age.

Quick Quote:

If we are not supposed

to eat animals, why are

they made of meat?

Anon

O

Odours in the Home

Yes, we're talking here about smelly old pensioners, who give off a fearful niff as they stagger about the house in their scruffy cardigans, food-stained shirts and carpet slippers. It's a vile lie, of course – old people are often more careful about personal cleanliness than many acned, booze-reeking youngsters. But, and it is a but I use carefully: old people's houses do smell a bit different. No?

Think back to when you were young and went on a duty visit to your granny. Don't you recall the very special smell that exuded from each room? Lavender, damp laundry (drying on a clothes horse in front of an open fire), pipe tobacco and, quite often, a disinfectant that could blind a horse at fifty paces. My own recollection, which is a bit hazy, because both my grannies snuffed it when I was still very young, is of baking smells, fresh bread, cakes and things like that. With all the family deodorants on the market today, I'm sure some smart marketing man could clean up if he produced a 'room freshener' that smelled of new-baked bread or home-made jam.

Fantasies apart, there is a tried and tested method to deodorise your home without resorting to expensive aerosol sprays or those slimy bits of rag sticking out of a jar that look like dead frogs without arms or legs. Try this way to rid your home of geriatric pongs: douse some cotton-wool balls in wintergreen oil (available in any good chemists or Harrods). Place these balls in the bathroom, kitchen and on the landing, if you have one. This done, hey presto, your home will smell like new. I've yet to try it, but wintergreen-soaked balls have a stupendous reputation among the cognoscenti, so do have a go. After all, those sprays and chemical deodorisers can cause allergies, whereas wintergreen is harmless.

So, in conclusion, when asked how you keep your house smelling so toasty fresh, you can answer 'It's all balls'.

Orange (the colour)

Old people should never wear anything orange. Apart from being the most horrible colour in the whole spectrum, you don't want to look like a tangerine on legs, do you?

Orgy

There have been alarming reports in recent years of old-age pensioners in the more affluent parts of the country becoming drawn to raucous party-going, where alcohol, loud music and sexual shenanigans are on offer in abundance. I take no moral stance over this, but I nevertheless advise those libidinous septuagenarians, octogenarians and nonagenarians, who are tempted to attend such gatherings, simply to say no.

A moment's reflection on what a roomful of naked old people in various states of tumescence actually look like should be enough for any sane person to turn these invitations down. I mean to say, just imagine somebody resembling Mother Teresa, Tony Benn or Ann Widdecombe naked, save for a garter belt, thong and stiletto heels, mounting (with or without sexual aids) a supine Bruce Forsyth lookalike transvestite. If that doesn't send a shudder down your spine, my friend, nothing will.

The word orgy derives from the Greek '*orgia*' which, roughly translated, means 'secret rites' or 'revels'. In the classical world, this included the worship of Bacchus, the God of Fertility and Wine. Don't let this historical association fool you into thinking it's OK. For us oldsters, prancing around without knickers to frenzied drumbeat and with naked strangers to whom we have not been properly introduced is a definite no-no. Sorry, but that's all there is to it. Try going to bed early, at home, with a good book. Almost any good book, except the *Kama Sutra*.

> **Quick Quote:**
>
> A young girl of eighteen
>
> is a coffer whose lock
>
> must be forced. A woman

of thirty is venison well

ripe and good to put on the spit.

A forty year old woman is a

great bastion where the cannon

has made more than one breach.

But at fifty, a woman is an old

lantern in which one places a

wick only with regret.

> Lois Petit de Bachaumont (Author and poet from
> the Court of Marie Antoinette and clearly a dirty,
> old, chauvinistic sod into the bargain)

Overseas Property

According to a recent survey, more than two million people in the
United Kingdom intend to buy property overseas in the near future.
A large proportion of them will be pensioners who will be, no
doubt, seeking to make their pensions go further by living in low-
cost, sunny Spain, France or even Florida.

It is very tempting for old folk who have paid off their mortgage to
realise some of the locked-in capital of their houses and zip over to
the continent on a house-hunting visit, organised often by a canny
estate agent who specialises in homes overseas. There are strong
arguments both in favour of making such a move and, of course,
counter arguments of equal force.

I write as one who has owned a house in Spain, purchased before
I retired, and I have experienced both the pluses and the minuses of
being an overseas property owner. While my wife and I never
intended to live permanently in Spain and we always retained our
house in England, we know many friends who have severed links with
the UK for a life in the sun. Each individual case is different, but
before embarking on such an adventure, and adventure it certainly is
for the over sixties, there are some simple rules which can minimise
the risks when purchasing that whitewashed villa with ocean views
and a mountain backdrop.

First of all, don't leave your brains at Heathrow or Gatwick. Many people do and by the time they alight on the tarmac of some Mediterranean airport, they are so seduced by the prospect of a home in the sun that they are suckers for the first smooth-talking property agent who comes across their path.

I have no wish to blacken the reputations of all Spanish, French, Portuguese or American estate agents, but please remember, crooks do exist. And they love old English people with money to burn. So the first thing you should do is contact the Association of International Property Professionals (AIPP). Its membership directory shows over 300 members who adhere to a code of professional conduct and integrity.

You should also obtain independent legal advice before you start out and check out both the developer and the agent of the property you are interested in. Don't buy off plan. This is my personal view. Your independent legal adviser may disagree, but there have been too many cases of fraud in recent years to make 'off-plan purchases'. A bit risky. Always visit the site. Check out the locality. How close are the shops, motorways, restaurants, etc.

See if there are plans for further developments that may spoil your view. This is a very common problem. Sign nothing, not even a deposit cheque, until you have cleared this with your lawyer. Check all charges that will accrue if you complete the purchase, i.e. local taxes, water and fuel rates, insurance, valid freehold status or clear leasehold arrangement.

If, in the end, you go ahead and splash out on that dream retirement home, please remember:

- You will be a foreigner in a foreign land.
- You will look ridiculous in shorts until your knees turn brown.
- You will look even more ridiculous if your knees turn red, swell and peel.
- Ditto your bald head.
- A little Spanish guitar music goes a long way.
- Watch your booze levels; many old people in their first flush of overseas property ownership drink themselves into oblivion.
- Try to avoid becoming part of an 'English ghetto'. You've chosen to be abroad, try mixing with the locals.

- And learn their language (even if it is American).

- Last but not least, don't spend all your savings or the whole proceeds of your UK house sale on your foreign property. And leave a few bob in your bank in England.

So there you are. The choice is yours. For me? I no longer own property abroad and as I never intended to live there permanently, I would only contemplate retiring abroad if I rented a place. Good luck and ole.

Having said watch your booze levels, after writing that, I dug out an old survey about alcohol and read that Dr Agnes Heinz, Director of Nutrition and Biochemistry at the American Council of Science and Health, says, 'The liver is an enormous recuperative organ and moderate drinkers can live longer than abstainers!'

Also, researchers at Harvard have concluded that a moderate intake of red wine helps to relieve stress and those who drink wine have twenty-five per cent less chance of having a heart attack.

So go carefully, you oldies on the Costa del Sol, but don't give up altogether!

Oxo

Apart being a fine additive to stews and pies, those little cubes have another excellent use. OK, so you have a flabby, baggy, horribly white old torso. You do, don't you? Be honest. You secretly long to look tanned, because a tan equals youthfulness, fitness and so forth.

No need to spend half your pension on visiting that tanning saloon next to the surgical appliance shop in the high street. No need at all. Simply pop a dozen Oxo cubes in a tub of soapy water, hop in and soak. Hey presto, a glowing golden tan that would be the envy of Peter Hain and Kilroy-Silk. (It's only fair to tell you that I wrote this after five double whiskies and an untipped Capstan, full strength, that I found in the attic.)

A word of warning, though; this fine new colour doesn't mean you can wear a thong on the beach or at the pool (see 'B' for Bottoms), but glimpses of your tanned chest through that nice white cotton shirt will be most impressive. Oh yes. Stay out of the rain.

Quick Quote:

I went up into the
attic with my mother-
in-law the other day –
filthy, smelly and
covered in cobwebs
but she's kind to the children.

Tommy Cooper

P

Packaging

Modern packaging is specifically designed to drive old people into a frenzy of despair. Why, they ask themselves, is it necessary for a pair of robust secateurs to be encased in a rubble of plastic so thick and so strong that you need a separate set of secateurs just open the damn thing?

When bringing your shopping home, most of which will be either in bulletproof plastic or airtight cling film, old people must have the following items to hand to facilitate the dread ceremony of – opening the purchases!

1. a saw

2. a blowtorch

3. a small axe

4. half an ounce of Semtex

5. a first-aid kit

6. a stiff drink

Only when this operation is complete can you load up your fridge, larder or kitchen shelves with the merchandise you have liberated from its packaging. Then, with a heavy heart and a gashed finger or two, you realise that lying on the kitchen table is a small mountain of waste plastic, paper and cling film that must, upon pain of prosecution or possibly death by stoning, be recycled into a special bin kindly provided by your local council.

You may note, while sorting all this junk into the appropriate piles, that a lot of the manufactures' packagers are so proud of their work that they print their names on their products. Some of them may even be British with company names like 'Sod Your Fingernails'.

Finally, it's not a bad idea when shopping at your local supermarket to play the 'helpless old buffoon' at the checkout and ask that nice girl with the nose ring to unpack all the stuff you've just bought from the trolley. You'd be surprised; a lot of them will, in fact, do it for you. But you have to look helpless and vulnerable. You can do vulnerable can't you?

Quick Quote:

'Pierce with a pin and push off'.

Instruction on a 1950s tin of

beans. After obeying these

instructions and running out

of the kitchen, I returned to

find a packet of dried peas

which urged me to even greater

feats of speed and endurance.

It bore the legend – 'tear along the dotted line'.

Jed Hurren

Patriotism

Patriotism is derived from the very ancient word *patrios*, which means 'of one's father'. Most of us, however, accept its modern meaning, which is to love one's country and to be devoted to its interests, especially its freedom and independence.

It is a tragedy of the twentieth century that this fine word has been hijacked by dubious extremists and used as a slogan to mask their true political intention. They have done much the same to both the Union flag and the English flag in particular. Worse still, modern cynics have dredged up the old canard that 'patriotism is the last refuge of a scoundrel', which I have always believed to be a dangerous and misleading statement.

Most people over sixty understand the true meaning of the word 'patriotism' and should, I believe, pass this intelligence down to younger generations and try to persuade them that devotion to the common weal, as the ancients used to say, is a wholly honourable thing.

To be proud of one's country is a noble emotion. But a word of caution: while we British don't need to be over demonstrative in our patriotism, quiet loyalty being the British way, wouldn't it be splendid if we showed a little more visible support to British servicemen and women returning from fields of conflict and celebrated the various British Saint's days with a flag or some other token of acknowledgement.

Or am I, and those of you who share my sentiments, no more than fusty old dinosaurs, who have failed to grasp the fact the world has moved on and the only time we should display any signs of patriotism is when we are drunk and at an international football match.

Quick Quote:

Clay lies still, but

blood's a rover, breath's

a ware that will not keep.

Up lad when the

journey's over there'll

be time enough to sleep.

A.E. Houseman

Political Correctness

What is political correctness? Is it a genuine phenomenon or merely a creation of the popular press? Is it a sort of catch-all phrase to enable headline writers to describe and attack some of the more ludicrous announcements and decrees pumped out by our political masters? Or is it a real, intellectual mindset that seeks to influence the way we live, speak and react with our fellow citizens?

For many older people, it is, indeed, a baffling phenomenon. They read instances of its poisonous effects on the way we conduct our everyday existence and ask: Who invented it? How did it come about? What is it for?

These are difficult questions to answer, but it is perhaps useful to remind ourselves that its origins were benign. The desire not to insult or belittle people of different races, religions or sexual orientation to ourselves. In short, it was about good manners, decency and politeness.

I shall pause here, while hordes of colonel blimps in the Shires turn purple with rage over their whisky and sodas.

However, in spite of its original intentions, if my analysis is correct, political correctness has become a weapon of control in the hands of the fascist/liberal establishment. Yes, I know that is a contradictory statement, but political correctness itself is full of contradictions. It seeks to free minorities from persecution in word and deed, but at its most extreme, merely stifles free speech and even opinions that do not conform to the current quasi-liberal consensus.

Many of the examples of 'political correctness gone mad' are familiar to older people, who have now moved beyond being amused by it and are genuinely concerned about its sinister, creeping agenda of brainwashing and control. Is that too extreme an analysis? I don't think so.

The peddlers of political correctness, who are usually officials of some sort or other, seek to demonise certain words of which they don't approve. They are also obsessed with what can only be described as 'risk avoidance', 'social inclusion' and 'the creation of a bland, grey, egalitarian desert of conformity'. But to a standard, *they set*, which we, on pain of legal sanction, must all conform to.

The growth of political correctness in our country has now reached almost Stalinist proportions and I use the word 'Stalinist' deliberately. When the free world faced down and defeated the odious plague of communism, we rejoiced. Little did we know that 'conformity, drab equality and mind control' would leak back onto the agenda of petty local officials and bureaucrats, who sought to introduce their warped vision of society by the back door.

To my fellow pensioners, crumblies, wrinklies and dodderers, I say, 'Reject all these blandishments from our so-called masters.' We don't need lessons in politeness or caring or instructions on how to behave. Neither will we accept that words and phrases we have used for decades quite freely should now be proscribed by jacks-in-office in Whitehall or the local town hall.

After all, that little rag doll you found in the attic long after your children left home is still called a golliwog and when you make a contribution freely to the charity St Dunstan's, it's not to help the 'visually impaired' or 'the sight disadvantaged', it is to help the blind.

Politics

There are only *ten* fundamental truths about politics with which most older people are familiar; however, just in case you are one of the few who isn't, here they are again in all their stark simplicity:

1. Elected politicians do not actually run the country. Civil Servants do and have done for centuries.

2. Whenever an elected politician actually tells the truth, the unvarnished, unambiguous truth, Landseer's Great Bronze Lions in Trafalgar Square let out a gigantic roar.

3. After a government cock-up, balls-up, screw-up or any other administrative disaster, government spokesmen will claim 'lessons have been learnt'. They haven't. They never, ever have been learnt; neither will they be as long as there is snow on Mount Kilimanjaro.

4. Most administrations end in tears rather than in triumph.

5. We do not live in a full democracy. Only a poor imitation of one.

6. The more the three main parties fight over who occupies the 'middle ground', the greater the chance of extremist groups from the loony left and the foaming right gaining support from disgruntled members of the electorate. Remember, nature abhors a vacuum.

7. Today's political debate is not between politicians and the people; it is almost exclusively between politicians and the media.

8. The media set the political agenda. Politicians only pretend to.

9. Multinationals in our country have more power and influence over employment levels than any government.

10. Within the next five to ten years, what remains of our sovereignty will be handed over to unelected bureaucrats in Brussels. Thus, exercising your vote in a British general election will have as much influence on how you are governed as King Canute did in stemming the incoming tide.

All the above may sound like gloomy prognostication. That's because it is. Sorry. Go and pour yourself a stiff drink before a future government introduces prohibition – you think I'm kidding? Don't hold your breath.

And while you sip your chosen alcoholic beverage, draw comfort from this one thought: whenever you think things can't get any worse, they invariably will.

Quick Quote:

Every politician needs

a Willy!

Margaret Thatcher (referring to William Whitelaw)

Posh

The origination of the word 'posh' is associated with long sea journeys on ocean liners, usually to and from the Far East. Very rich people in first-class accommodation chose to travel 'port out' and 'starboard home' for reasons that to me remain obscure. Less affluent passengers travelled in steerage or second class. So the 'posh out' and 'starboard home' became abbreviated to posh.

The word has since become grossly misused and deployed largely to attack anybody whose intelligence, accent or education is higher than that of a sea anemone. This is a form of insult, which has proliferated in the age of the common man. There was a time, in my youth, when a cultivated accent, i.e. standard English, was a thing to aspire to. Today, unless you waffle in estuary English, with glottal stops and dropped aitches, you are condemned as posh.

Old people should not be fooled into thinking this attitude is 'democratic' and thus makes speech more 'inclusive' and 'accessible'. It doesn't. It is just inverted snobbery (see 'S' for speech). And it is not necessary to have been to a public school to speak good English. Think of Richard Burton or Sir Roger Moore.

We old people must set an example to the young and hopefully reverse the trend that glorifies sloppy pronunciation and grammar. So don't just sit there gasping at the semi-literate mumblings of some overpaid celebrity on the telly that your grandchildren mimic, do something about it. Tell them that English is a language of the business world, the language of Shakespeare and Shaw and Wilde. Tell them that good spoken and written English is the best artillery you can have in life.

Quick Quote:

I haven't spoken

to my wife for six

weeks. I thought

it impolite to interrupt.

Mike Reid

Primal Scream (for old-age pensioners)

If you've not tried it and you'd like to, pick your moment with care. A primal scream will reduce your inner tensions wonderfully and after performing it, you will feel cleansed. Warn your partner, though. Some primal screamers have been struck on the head with blunt instruments by their wives/husbands, who thought they were having a noisy tantrum.

Here are the rules to observe if you want to obtain the most benefit from a primal scream:

1. Go outside

2. Take a deep breath

3. Scream

4. Keep screaming till your hair stands on end and you go boss-eyed

5. Stop

6. Go inside and have a small drink

7. Prepare yourself for the phone calls from the neighbours, especially those who have contacted the police or ambulance service.

8. Explain jocularly to any caller that you were just having a primal scream for medical purposes and offer to let them join you next time.

9. Put your house up for sale

10. Next time you scream, wear a false nose, beard and sunglasses.

> **Quick Quote:**
>
> A doctor said to his
>
> 80-year-old lady patient,
>
> 'You've got acute
>
> angina.' She blushed
>
> and said, 'Thanks doctor,
>
> but I haven' taken my
>
> knickers off yet.'

Anon

Prostate

OK, another cringe-inducing subject, but here goes. For those of us, all male, who have waited with trepidation while our doctor snaps on the rubber glove as a prelude to what is quaintly described as an 'internal investigation', will know that this is a necessary humiliation that we must bear with fortitude. My only complaint is to ask why it is necessary for the doctor to engage you in a totally banal conversation while executing this procedure.

Just consider, do you really want to discuss Manchester United's chances in the European Cup, while a younger man has his index finger rammed up your arse? If you do, that's fine with me; we live in a free and liberal society.

Personally, I prefer no idle chit-chat during the procedure or, at best, the soothing strains of Beethoven's Fifth ... Or you could paraphrase the remark made by an aristocratic lady in the thirties who, when asked by her hairdresser how she would like her hair done, replied, 'In complete silence, please.'

Q

The Queen (HM)

God bless her. Even if you are a Republican, just consider the alternative for a moment. Neil Kinnock? John Major? Tony Blair, Jeffrey Archer? Elton John? Right that's enough. Horrible, isn't it.

Even if we do eventually become a republic and a new president is appointed, or elected, my vote would be for Mrs Elizabeth Windsor, if she's still knocking around. After that? Maybe I won't be here to see it. How about you?

Politicians these days are regarded with such disdain, even loathing, that a non-partisan head of state is about the last focus we have as a nation to encourage a sense of unity and belonging.

Finally, here is a curious finding from a recent academic study. It concluded after months of erudite research that there are just five Christian or forenames that are completely unacceptable in a head of state. I prefix them each with a title, so you can get the flavour of the academics' conclusions:

King	Reg
President	Beryl
King	Clint
President	Tracey
Queen	Cherie

It's a funny old world, eh?

Quick Quote:

After a hard day's
reigning there's
nothing the Queen
likes more than a
nice cup of tea.

The Queen Mother (allegedly)

Queuing

I think it is fair to say that we British oldies invented queuing. I have been unable, in spite of exhaustive research, to discover an intellectually robust history of queuing. So much of what I am now writing is based upon anecdotal evidence.

Although there were lines of people in New York during the Depression waiting to receive their bowl of soup from the hastily convened soup kitchens, they were not, in the strict sense of the word, 'queuing'. A cursory glance at old press cuttings from the *Wall Street Journal* or the *New York Times* shows faded sepia photographs of men and women in shabby overcoats, sort of hanging around in wiggly lines. They were not queuing. They might have been 'waiting in line', a curious transatlantic expression still in use today, but, all together now, 'they were not queuing'.

Queuing, British-style, i.e. proper queuing, is a precise and unique form of behaviour. The first recorded incident of perfect queuing was in 1946 in London, in a small street that ran parallel with Fulham Road in SW6. Here, it was observed by a noted social historian (i.e. my dad that seventy-nine women wearing headscarves were queuing outside Mr Shepherd's grocery store, all clutching ration books in one hand and carrying Woodbines between the index and second finger of the other hand. (The shopping basket would be looped over the crook of the arm that extended to the hand that held the ration book.)

Only three phrases escaped these women's lips as they queued and Dad took careful note of what they were. His pencilled notes, alas, have long perished, but not before he passed the intelligence on to me. The three phrases, uttered by all the women at different intervals, were:

1. A bit nippy for this time of the year.

2. My feet are killing me.

3. Mustn't grumble.

Now, there is a clear lesson to be drawn from these remarkable snatches of conversation; indeed, an iron lesson for all queuing aficionados. The primary, nay the only, two subjects that are permitted to be discussed while performing the ancient queuing ritual are the state of the 'queuees' feet and the weather. All other topics are forbidden.

The third item 'mustn't grumble' is the absolute proof that the queue is a British invention. 'Mustn't grumble', a simple phrase that is redolent with meaning, a phrase that encapsulates the British character. No matter how dire the circumstances or how long the queue, we 'mustn't grumble'.

Don't you feel a stab of pride when you hear these words? They have been passed down from generation to generation, like sacred icons. Sadly, today's youngsters, no doubt influenced by stampeding hordes at pop concerts or foreign immigrants hammering on the glass doors of Selfridges during autumn sales week, have lost the true art of queuing.

It is therefore a solemn duty of us older people to teach our youngsters just how to do it properly. A queue is a social occasion, but a very serious one, where patience, aching feet and faintly ironic remarks about the climate are fused into one glorious whole, giving the queue itself a noble, almost balletic significance. Let the Americans, the Serbo-Croats, the Chinese and the Russians stand in line, raggedly and impatiently, chattering inanely about everything under the sun, except the weather; let them jostle and push and try to sneak up a few places. Let them, because they don't know how to queue. We, with our stern discipline, sense of order, acute sensitivity to changes in temperature and genuine concern over foot health, are an example to lesser breeds.

A wag once observed that British people have been known to join the end of a queue even when they had no idea what the queue was for. They had seen a queue and with instincts honed over decades, they knew that it was their duty to join it. Just writing these words causes an opalescent tear to course down my cheek. Makes you proud, doesn't it.

R

Research (I)

The word 'research' covers a multitude of activities, some of which are vital, others completely useless and a few merely of fleeting interest. The most important 'research' is that which is followed by the words 'and development'.

Most responsible industries and, indeed, governments invest a great deal of money in R & D and it is from this noble and essential activity that many new products, medical innovations and services spring. Most of us accept that the pharmaceutical industry has to apportion a huge part of its income for research and that developing new medicines, for example, is a long process that will reflect on the price we finally pay for our drugs, cough mixtures and headache remedies.

Much the same criteria apply to the defence, energy and nuclear industries which must, if they are to keep pace with demand and competition, constantly innovate and improve. So far so good, you might say. What about 'useless' research mentioned at the top of this section? The most 'useless' and sometimes dangerous research is that commissioned by lazy tabloid editors, who use it when they seem unable to fill their newspapers with 'real' news. How often have you opened your daily rag to read that 'a recent survey showed that three out of five ginger-haired clergymen living in Nottingham have never boiled an egg for more than six minutes'?

OK. OK. You've never read such an item, but you get my drift. The most pernicious thing about these 'surveys' is how often they change their findings and conclusions. Not that long ago, 'research' suggested that 'we should go to work on an egg', i.e. eggs are good for you. Now, too many, apparently, are not good for you.

The other thing we oldies should keep a weather eye on is the statistics that accompany these spurious surveys. Let me cite an imaginary example of how statistics can be both true and at the same time grossly misleading: a survey in the year 2000 states that one per cent (i.e. one in one hundred) of people over of sixty-five are likely to develop ingrowing toenails. A survey the following year in 2001 states that new research now shows that two per cent (i.e. two in each hundred) of people over the age of sixty-five is likely to develop ingrowing toenails. The tabloid editor seizes upon this and his blazing headline reads:

Ingrowing toenail epidemic among 65-year-olds. A recent survey shows the number of oldsters suffering from this awful condition has doubled in a year!

While this is true that, statistically, the number has doubled from one per cent to two per cent, both figures, allowing for margins of error in calculations, are utterly meaningless. Extrapolate for a moment. If last year ten people in every 1,000 developed dodgy toenails and this year twenty in every 1,000 did, would this be cause for concern? To be honest, research like this is just fodder for rubbish headlines or dud ammunition for lazy journalists to fire at us, the consuming public.

That splendid writer Keith Waterhouse has labelled most government research as either 'stating the bleeding obvious' or having emanated from the 'Department of Guesswork'. Right on the button, Keith. Right on the button.

Now for the controversial bit. Research into smoking and health (see also 'S' for smoking). Let me state an interest. I am a cigar smoker, about 3–4 a week; fairly light consumption, I think you might agree. But I am nonetheless a user of the Lady Nicotine. I used to smoke twenty-five cigarettes a day, but gave up forty years ago. Even then, however, I knew cigarettes were not good for me. At the age of sixteen, we called them 'cancer sticks'. We were fully aware of what we were doing and we knew that regular puffing could impair our health, but what we didn't know, and wouldn't have cared much if we had, was that a zealous and puritanical organisation called ASH (Action Against Smoking and – presumably 'for' – Health) was going to spring up not only to 'state the bleeding obvious', but to actually use untruths in their propaganda. (OK, half-truths.)

Do I exaggerate? I think not. On ciggy packets, we now have the direst warnings like 'Smoking Kills' or 'Smokers Die Young'. The clear implication of these bald statements is that 'all smokers die young' and that smoking *will* kill you. I'm sorry, folks, this is just not true. The words, if truth is what you seek, should run as follows: 'Some Smokers Die Young' and 'Smoking Can Kill You'.

Come on, let's face it, did Churchill die young? Or George Burns? Or countless others? Of course they didn't.

I'll pause here while you grind your teeth in anger at the last paragraph.

OK, let me put my case bluntly. I accept, totally, the ban on smoking in public places, restaurants, theatres, aeroplanes, etc., and I accept the evidence that smoking can be harmful. Notice that word 'can', it is important. What I don't understand is why ASH and other anti-smoking zealots have to use weasel words in their attacks on smokers. We smokers accept their broad findings, we really do. They don't have to lie or dissemble. Especially about passive smoking.

Passive smoking – allow me two last controversial statements on the subject:

1. There is not any conclusive evidence that passive smoking *kills*. (Annoys, maybe, but kills, no way.)

2. Non-smokers die every day.

Sorry if I've upset you. I would never attempt to smoke in your presence or in a non-smoking environment, honest I wouldn't.

But we live in a free society. Having been warned in near hysterical terms about the dangers of smoking, we old people would now like to make our own judgements about whether the risks outweigh the pleasure or vice versa. Being nagged by purse-lipped puritans and patronising politicians will only cause our blood pressure to soar and that really is dangerous.

Quick Quote:

W.C. Fields was once

refused an insurance claim

for a small fire that occurred

in his bedroom, as the

insurance company said

he must have caused the

fire himself by smoking in

bed, to which W.C. replied,

'nonsense, the bed was

already alight when I got

into it'.

Probably Apocryphal

Research (II) (Other)

And by 'other' research, I mean surveys, opinion polls and men in raincoats with clipboards stopping you in the street and asking about your sex life.

First of all, if you are part of a research project, one of say 1,000 people in a sample, you must lie, regardless of the subject. Oh yes. Great big whoppers, if you please. Here's a specimen based on a real survey conducted recently in a town where I live. The earnest young man with a clipboard was anxious to get my 'take' on 'sex and alcohol'. Truly. Here's how the interview went:

> YOUNG MAN   How many units of alcohol do you drink in a week?
>
> ME   I don't drink units. I pour booze in copious quantities down my throat seven days a week.
>
> Y.M.   *After a pause and a quizzical stare* A unit is a glass of wine. So how many do you think you consume in a week?
>
> ME   Six hundred and forty-two.
>
> Y.M.   *Despairingly* Does this affect your sex life?
>
> ME   Yes.
>
> Y.M.   How?
>
> ME   I can no longer copulate while standing up in a hammock.
>
> Y.M.   I don't think you're being serious, sir.
>
> ME   You're a very perceptive young man, good day to you.
>
> Y.M.   Thank you, sir.

Moments later, because I have the hearing of a bat, I heard the young man muttering, 'Silly old git.'

Game, set and match, I think!

A lot of questionnaires that drop through your letterbox are full of impertinent questions that you should refuse to answer. They are usually from manufacturers who want to sell you something. Then there are quasi-official ones from the local council or some other interfering bunch of busybodies. Some even contain thinly veiled threats about how you will be fined £1,000 if you don't fill them in.

I particularly loathe those which ask you to name your 'partner'. I cross 'partner' out and write 'wife'. The government, both local and national, the DVLA, the Inland Revenue and the Registrar of Births, Deaths and Marriages have all the possible data on you that can be reasonably expected in a modern society. So when you are asked to fill in yet another complex form, scrawl across it: 'None of your bloody business', put it in an envelope and mark it 'Return to Sender'.

Finally, at the time of writing, the prospect of identity cards being imposed on us grows almost daily. With the government's track record on previous computer-based data collection schemes being so utterly hopeless, it seems a moral duty for us older people to say 'Stop. No further'. If enough of us refuse to cooperate, the whole ghastly shambles will have to be abandoned.

Retirement Homes

Sometimes called 'care homes' and occasionally 'old folk's homes', they usually have twee names like Sunset Lodge or Safe Haven, although in Texas, USA, there is a popular geriatric resting place that rejoices in the name of 'The Last Redoubt'.

Whatever they are called and wherever they are located, if you are over sixty, you should make it your business to check out a few of them near to where you live now. Just in case. Yes, I know it's usually your children or even your grandchildren who are the ones to pick your retirement home, but it doesn't do any harm to have done a bit of research beforehand.

Before my late mother went into a 'care home' over twenty-five years ago, my wife and I had looked at a few and, of course, they varied in quality and acceptability as I'm sure they still do today.

When I was young, my image of an old folk's home was not a particularly benign one. With my overheated imagination, I thought they'd be a cross between a Victorian lunatic asylum and the sort of clinic featured in that magnificent Jack Nicholson movie *One Flew Over the Cuckoo's Nest.*

Today, the very best are like luxury hotels and the worst, just a notch above bedlam. So, if you want to avoid ending up sitting cross-legged in a pool of your own urine doing basket weaving, while Nazi Storm Troopers force-feed you squirrel soup and inject your buttocks with horse tranquillisers, here's a checklist of questions to ask if you are visiting a care home, both before admission and perhaps on behalf of those old folk who are already resident:

1. Reception. How were you greeted? Was the atmosphere warm and inviting? Was it pleasantly furnished and decorated? How did it smell?

2. Did the residents look contented or miserable? Did they look clean and properly dressed? Were the rooms light and cheerful? Did the residents seem socially compatible, i.e. did they chat to each other or read or watch television?

3. Did the home allow personal possessions, i.e. favourite ornaments, bits of furniture, etc., to soften the institutional atmosphere of the place?

4. Were the staff friendly and properly dressed, i.e. no jeans and dirty trainers? Were they qualified? Just ask. Don't be shy.

5. Are activities organised properly, i.e. outings and visits? Are residents' celebrated?

6. Was there a garden or space outside, so the residents could enjoy a bit of fresh air?

7. Were the toilets and bathroom areas *scrupulously* clean? I mean really pristine. Dirty loos are an indicator that the rest of the home is likely to be sub-standard.

8. How was the food? Ask the residents. Try to get a peek at the kitchen.

9. Make sure the home has a local authority licence to operate (if it is private).

10. Ask yourself, 'Could I see myself or one of my loved ones living here in reasonable comfort?'

And when you leave the home, say a little prayer and hope that you'll never need one.

Quick Joke:

What do you get if you

cross a Jehovah's Witness

with a Hell's Angel?

A bloke who knocks at

your door on Sunday

morning and tells you

to sod off.

Royal Jelly

Supposed to be very good for old people, some say it can prolong life. Even if it doesn't, a regular ingestion of the stuff can't do any harm.

The drawback, of course, is that it is very expensive. When I asked a nice man in Harrods why it was so pricey, he gave me a world-weary smile and explained that actually, 'getting hold of it' was 'jolly complicated'.

'A bit like getting caviar from sturgeons,' I suggested.

'Not exactly,' came the reply. 'Royal Jelly is a substance secreted by the pharyngeal glands of worker bees and fed to all larvae when very young and to larvae destined to become Queens through their development.'

Of course, silly of me not having known that. I mean to say, grabbing a handful of worker bees and draining their pharyngeal glands in enough quantities to fill a jam jar can't be an easy job.

However, in spite of the cost, and the difficulty of supply, if you are an old person (and you are, aren't you?) and you've got a few bob to spare, have a go at the old Royal Jelly. I can tell you this; it tastes better than Beluga Caviar, which only has the flavour of fish.

Quick Joke:

What does a 75-
year-old woman
have between her
breasts that a 25-
year-old doesn't?
Her navel.

Anon

S

School

Revisiting your old school can be an experience charged with emotion and nostalgia for many people. For others, it may remind them of unhappy times best forgotten. This piece, therefore, is aimed at the former, for those who recall those halcyon days through the proverbial pink-tinted glasses.

It matters not a jot whether your schooling was at Eton or Bog Lane Comprehensive, if you remember it fondly, a visit is always worthwhile.

For me, although the old building in Chelsea, where I received my education, still stands 'twixt the Fulham Road and trendy Kings Road, it is no longer the raffish, bohemian grammar school it once was. It is now a rather prim adult education centre that seems to specialise in social-awareness classes and citizenship seminars. Once, the classrooms rang to the babble of young London voices reciting Shakespeare badly, but with extraordinary brio. Now, those same hallowed rooms, minus the scarred and ink-stained desks, reverberate to the hum of politically correct nostrums about 'inconclusiveness' and 'accessibility'. History, if it is taught at all, I have no doubt will have been scrubbed up and be heavy on post-imperial guilt and reappraisals.

These horrors apart, it was still wonderful to see the old place again and remember the extraordinary masters who managed to drum a certain amount of sense and literacy into the heads of a bunch of scrofulous, rough-mannered, working-class kids. Meeting old school chums, too, was a remarkable experience. Men one hadn't set eyes on for over half a century, my goodness, how they had aged! Did they think the same about me? Go on, take a wild guess.

How different our life paths had been. Some had achieved spectacular success, going on to university and then climbing the corporate ladder in business; others had achieved fame as well-known thespians or high-flyers in the civil service. A few had been content to remain within their proletarian milieu, but were nonetheless happy and content with their lot. In short, most of the old boys I met were well adjusted, philosophical and comfortable in their own skins.

So do try to visit your old school. The ghosts of those old masters and the spirits of old school chums long dead will stalk the corridors, but they will be happy ghosts, reminding you of that time of innocence and discovery that is so quickly tarnished by the emergence into the adult world.

If, like me, your school was situated slap-bang next to a girl's grammar school, you will recall the extraordinary rush of emotion when you realised that those grubby creatures in gymslips would emerge from the chrysalis of childhood to become gorgeous objects of desire that would put the final touches to your education.

Self-assessment

It is very important for old people to conduct a critical analysis of themselves from time to time in order to avoid being mocked by others for 'not acting your age'. Now this is a very delicate matter and must be approached with both caution and rigour. To begin with, one must take a leap of faith and ask, ruthlessly, am I doing any of the following things?

1. Am I wearing inappropriately tight clothes?

2. Do I hold my stomach in on a beach when members of the opposite sex stroll by?

3. Do I go to a gym frequented mostly by younger people?

4. When at the gym, do I wear Lycra and a ludicrous sweatband round my forehead?

5. Do I dance at my children or grandchildren's parties?

6. Do I snore while watching television?

7. When breaking wind in company, do I cough noisily to mask the sound?

8. Do I try to be cool by using phrases like 'hey man' or 'awesome'?

9. Do I know the words of the latest pop song? (Even worse, do I still know the words to all of Cliff Richard's hits?)

10. Do I read *Hello* and cancel my subscription to *Saga Magazine*?

11. Do I have my tongue pierced, my buttocks tattooed or my hair dyed? (Or, alternatively, my head shaved and my scrotum dyed orange?)

12. Do I go to Ibiza in high summer and 'hit the clubs'?

13. Do I pretend to like takeaway pizzas?

14. Do I deny all knowledge of drinking Babycham in my youth?

15. Do I pretend to hate Rolf Harris?

16. Have I thrown away all my Fair Isle sweaters or, if a lady, have I burned my bra?

17. Do I claim that my sexual appetite is as voracious as Casanova's?

18. Do I laugh heartily (and falsely) at 'alternative' young comedians, whose routines consist entirely of jokes about their genitalia, excrement, vomiting and how Mrs Thatcher was a fascist cow?

19. Do I pretend to actively give a toss about Britney Spears' marital troubles?

20. Am I behaving, in short, like a prat?

Quick Quote:

Queen Elizabeth the
First was bald and had
wooden teeth and yet,
miraculously managed
to remain a virgin.

Jack Dee

Sex

Oops, it's slipped in again, if you'll pardon the expression.

I have only two pieces of advice under this heading, you will no doubt be mightily relieved to hear. First, for the ladies: always be on top. And I mean always. You don't want your partner to snuff it while he's hammering away, do you? Think of the embarrassment of having that dead weight (literally) pinning you to your Slumberland. Imagine having to phone a neighbour or worse, a fork-lift truck operator to come and help shift him. Nasty. So on top, girls. No compromises.

Secondly, you old fellows: don't even try; send out for a younger man wearing jackboots, a black silk shirt and very short hair.

Quick Quote:

P.J. O'Rourke was

right when he said no

one ever had a fantasy

about being tied to a

bed and sexually

ravished by someone

dressed as a Liberal.

Sleep

Ah – perchance to dream! Sleeping is now one of my most favourite pastimes. I am lucky enough to enjoy a solid eight hours' kip most nights and, I am not ashamed to admit, an afternoon nap as well. Old people often complain they sleep less as they grow older, but this is usually because they are less physically active than they were when they were younger and they spoil their chances of a good night's rest by sporadic dozing or 'nodding off' in a random fashion. You can spot a random 'nodder-off' quite easily, as he or she will usually accompany their snooze by dribbling down their chin or releasing pathetic snuffling noises. It is therefore best to avoid this unlovely practice if you are trying to improve your night-sleeping patterns.

Difficult sleepers may be suffering from mild insomnia, which is common among the sixty-plus brigade. Doctors say that if it takes you more than forty-five minutes to get off to sleep and then you wake frequently, you are an insomniac.

My doctor's advice is pretty straightforward:

1. Try to avoid sleeping pills. They can be habit forming.

2. Take a warm bath before retiring.

3. Don't eat, read or watch TV in bed. Bed is for sleeping ... OK, and rumpy pumpy, you lecherous old fool.

4. Sleep at a regular time each night.

5. Go to bed only when you feel sleepy.

6. Rise at the same time each day

Only when you have established a satisfactory sleeping pattern at night should you take this afternoon nap.

I must admit, I don't always follow my doctor's advice and I find a glass of brandy before bed quite helpful. Other people may find alcohol last thing at night too much of a stimulant. You can easily find out the routine that suits you best and like most things recommended for old people, routine and regularity are paramount.

Finally, a fashion tip. Men, throw away those hideous orange-and-black striped woollen jobs with the open fly and get a sexy, bright yellow silk pair of Cossack-style pyjamas – the ones with black piping round the edges. Will this help you sleep? Not necessarily, but if by unfortunate chance you snuff it during the night, then at least when the undertakers come to haul you off to the mortuary, you will go in style. You want to go in style, don't you?

And ladies. Something silky or satiny, if you please. Black or pink is good. With lace. Just imagine the shame of slipping off this mortal coil in a winceyette nightdress and a pair of old knickers. Dying with your hair in curlers is just adding insult to injury. I am told that in fashionable parts of London, like Knightsbridge, upmarket undertakers won't touch a female corpse unless she's wearing Gucci or Yves St Laurent.

So, ladies and gents, climb into bed well prepared. Sweet dreams.

Slogans

While most dictionaries describe a slogan as being derived from the Gaelic *sluagh-ghairm* or the war-cry of the old highland clans, its modern interpretation suggests a catchy advertising phrase or political statement.

I've never been sure whether a slogan is the same as a 'saw' which Cassell's Dictionary describes as a proverb or familiar maxim. Well, whatever, as young people say, my own parents were full of 'saws' and 'slogans'. And I am willing to wager a sack of diamonds to a pinch of salt that if you – dear reader – are over sixty-five you, too, will have inherited a bunch of old sayings that you will pass on to your children or grandchildren. Many are familiar, even commonplace. For example, I sure you have encountered the following:

- Look before you leap
- A stitch in time saves nine
- A fool and his money are soon parted
- Penny wise, pound foolish
- Don't judge a book by its cover
- And, of course, Shakespeare's 'All that glisters is not gold' (*The Merchant of Venice*, Act Two, Scene Six.)

In Shakespeare's *The Merchant of Venice*, Act Two, Scene Six, Portia's three suitors are asked to select one of three caskets – gold, silver and lead; one of them contains Portia's portrait and thus, whoever chooses it will win the lady's hand. Of course, Bassamo, her true love, picks the right one (lead), but the Prince of Morocco goes for gold and it's worth repeating his despairing speech in full:

Oh Hell, what have we here, a carrion death within whose empty eye there is a written scroll. I'll read the writing:

'All that glisters is not Gold

Often have you heard that told

Many a man his life has sold

But my outside to behold

Gilded tombs do worms enfold.

Had you been as wise as bold

Young in limbs in judgement old

Your answer had not been enscrolled.

Fare you well, your suit is cold'.
There are dozens of them, passed down from generation to generation, and many of them are rooted on that rare modern commodity, common sense.

The British Army has many, my favourite being the mantra of the SAS – 'Who Dares Wins'. But one has stayed with me since I encountered it in the 1950s as a young British officer in Vienna, with all its temptations, a burgeoning nightlife, cheap booze and pretty women. It was offered to me by my very stern commanding officer, Lieutenant Colonel John Willoughby (who later becomes Major General Sir John Willoughby) and I think it is a knockout. Probably originating among American Indians, the Sioux, perhaps, –'He who hoots with the owls at night cannot fly with the eagles at dawn'.

Every man and woman over sixty-five should have their own personal slogan. Do you?

Smoking

If you are over sixty-five, have smoked all your life and the only ill-effect is the occasional fall of soot, there is no advice I or your doctor can possibly give you. Don't be bullied by the health fascists, either.

That splendid old American comedian, the late George Burns, was once interviewed by a very PC young lady on CBS television. She expressed horror when he admitted that at the age of ninety-two, he smoked five big cigars a day. 'What does your doctor say?' she gasped.

'My doctor's dead,' said George with a benign smile, 'and he was a non-smoker.'

Pipes: young men smoke pipes in the hope it will give them an air of maturity, although these days it's rare to see anybody smoking a pipe. The old people who are pipe smokers often continue sucking away long after the thing has gone out, or never put any tobacco in it in the first place.

A psychiatrist friend of mine, who is himself clinically insane, tells me that sucking on an empty pipe is a substitute for the maternal nipple. So now you know, you disgusting old retard.

Quick Quote:

I have every sympathy

With the man who was

so horrified by what he

read about smoking,

that he gave up reading.

Groucho Marx

Sneezing

Old people tend to sneeze a lot and not simply because they are suffering from colds. I find a good bout of sneezing first thing in the morning clears the head wonderfully and sets me up for the rest of the day: seven heavy sneezes seems to do the trick, whereas five is too little and eight somewhat excessive. The general medical view of sneezing is pretty straightforward.

Don't hold back. Let it rip. Sneezing releases viruses and bacteria and this can only be a good thing. Stifling a sneeze not only makes you go cross-eyed, but may infect your sinuses and possibly cause, in extreme cases, mild ear infections. However, don't sneeze over or at other people. Sneeze with your mouth open, but covered with your hand or a handkerchief.

The best description of a sneeze I've ever read was written by the late Patrick Campbell. It is such a perfect description that I can do no better than reproduce part of it for your delectation. It is part of an essay Paddy wrote entitled *The Stallion Sneeze*. To set the scene, Paddy tells us that he has just plonked a peppered tomato, whole, into his mouth. He then goes on:

> First this giant force got to work upon my jaws and mouth, pressing out and hardening the delicate machinery until with the teeth bared and the upper lip drawn back, I must have looked like Silver the Mad Stallion about to do something unpleasant. At the same time, this frightful pressure squeezed my eyes shut and then shoved them along the Eustachian tubes into my ears, where they flung themselves against the drums, trying to get out.

This displacement of the eyes led immediately to a change in the shape of the top of my head.

It began to rise into a point, with the subsidiary effect of drawing me right up into the top left-hand corner of my high backed chair, so that it seemed that I retained a grip upon the floor only with a single toe. For some time, I held this pose, levitating, teeth bared, lips curled, nostrils flaring, eyes gone, ears bursting and nails dug deep into the upholstery. Then everything blew up.

Later in the piece, Paddy goes on:

The extremely high velocity of the breakfast tomato had enabled it to reach and penetrate every corner and crevice of the room. It was on the door, the ceiling and the four walls. It was in the typewriter. It had even struck a portrait of me painted by an aunt of mine in 1954 where it had obliterated one eye.

All I can say after reading that sublime piece for the hundredth time and still laughing is – Atishoo!

Quick Quote:

It now takes me

all night to do

what I used to

do all night.

> Allegedly Hugh Hefner
> (founder of *Playboy* Magazine)

Speech

It is speech, or the spoken language, that really separates us from the rest of the animal kingdom. It is sad, therefore, to note, with a patient shrug and a weary sigh, that in modern Britain, both vocabulary and speech are declining in quality.

Old people will recall how once, in a golden period of our Island history, BBC announcers spoke in clear, standard English. This was neither 'upper crust' nor 'chirpy chav'. The occasional soft Irish burr, Scottish lilt or Welsh sing-song was also acceptable. But in all cases, the words were clearly and properly pronounced. The 'H's' were sounded where they should have been, the endings of words, particularly 'ing', were not clipped off and grotesquely tortured phrases such as 'I was like, real cool' were quite unknown.

Today, the poison of sloppy speech has permeated even the highest in the land. What is to be done? More to the point, what are we fastidious crumblies going to do about it? When the shrill chorus of 'nothing' dies away, let me offer just one piece of advice: by speaking clearly and avoiding the more excruciatingly hideous phraseology of the 'celebrity' world, we may just set an example that our grandchildren may follow. But don't hold your breath.

Rebuking young people when they make clumsy mistakes in either pronunciation or grammar can sound patronising, even pompous. Don't, therefore, fall into this trap, lest your beloved grandchildren mark you down as a dithering pedant. Or worse.

Do, however, adopt an expression of quizzical disbelief, when a fractured, ill-pronounced sentence is uttered and ask politely if the speaker might care to repeat themselves, slowly. Pretending you cannot understand the precise meaning of what has been said often forces the person who uttered the offending words to rephrase them. In my experience, this works wonders and you, the old pedant, have not patronised or insulted the speaker, but required them to reformulate their language in a way that is more comprehensible. Do try it. But not on that Neanderthal, tattooed oaf who has just scraped your car when he utters, or rather grunts, the immortal phrase, 'git aht a me way, grannad.' And when relating the incident later at home, don't for God's sake say 'I was like, furious, nar mean?'

Spots

Spots. Yes, really, and we are not talking about teenage pimples here or acne, but those spots that come with age, usually on the back of the hands of old people.

My mother used to call them 'liver spots', for reasons I have never been able to fathom, but they are certainly unsightly. The American

132

comedian George Burns once said that if all the age spots on his body joined up, he'd have a permanent all-over tan.

If your hands are already dotted with the little perishers, there is only a limited amount you can do to alleviate the situation. Age spots are dark, purplish blemishes caused by the haemorrhaging of tiny blood vessels under the skin and there are cosmetic creams available at your pharmacy which will mask them.

However, recent studies in England have revealed that elderly people with age spots have a low level of zinc in their bodies. When zinc levels were increased, the age spots faded and in some cases, disappeared altogether. So look at your diet, you spotty ones, and include zinc-rich foods in your meals. They include seafood, onions, soya beans, spinach and whole grains. You can also purchase zinc tablets from your chemist or health food shop to supplement your diet, although it's worth asking your doctor before you do so.

Stairlifts

You can tell the age profile of a newspaper or magazine readership by looking at the advertisements. Any publication that has more than two separate stairlift advertisements is read by 65-year-olds. Any publication that has four or more separate stairlift advertisements is read by 80-year-olds. Any publication that has no advertisements other than those extolling the virtues of stairlifts is read by the undead.

The ads, for some reason, really annoy me. There's usually a grinning granny in twinset and pearls perched in what looks like a mini-ski-lift and at the foot of the stairs stands a grinning grandpa in a cardigan with a pipe stuck in his mouth.

Why are they looking so cheerful? If they can't manage the stairs, why don't they buy a bungalow? OK, that was cruel. When my wife reads that, I'll probably get a smack. But come on, folks. Is having an escalator in your home a cause for celebration and pipe smoking?

OK. OK, that's cruel, too. I must stop it. But listen, nipping up and down stairs or even moving gently up and down stairs is very good for old people. Unless they are really ill. Good for the leg muscles, the lungs and their circulation.

Oh, alright, I will accept, with my usual sour grace, that a stairlift can be a boon to those of us who really can't manage a short flight of stairs without pain. But is it necessary to wear a twinset and pearls and grin?

Is it permissible to use one of the contraptions, say, in frayed trousers and baggy T-shirt? Or dressed as Napoleon, frowning? Or naked?

I only asked.

Sunday

Sunday is, for old-age pensioners, the best day of the week. No question. Why? Because it means you've survived another week and tomorrow, Monday, is the start of the rest of your life.

I have a friend, (he's over seventy) who claims Wednesday is the best day of the week, but I reckon he's one sandwich short of a picnic. So go for Sunday, folks, nothing else comes close.

Quick Quote:

The first thing I do in

the morning is read the

obituary column in *The*

Times'. If I'm not in

it, I get up.

Harold Macmillan (when Prime Minister)

Swearing (Cursing, Oaths, etc.)

Since D. H. Lawrence's *Lady Chatterley's Lover* printed the 'F' word and Kenneth Tynan uttered it on live television, swearing has lost a lot of its potency. When we were young, a swear word was designed to shock, to punctuate the atmosphere with a jolt of electricity. A mother would order her child to 'wash its mouth out' if it uttered even a mild 'bloody'.

Today, the language of the barracks is commonplace across all classes of society. I adopt no moral stance over this issue, having worked for thirty-three years in commercial television. I would be a hypocrite if I did. But, whereas in my youth, a ripe oath, well chosen and sparingly used, was almost toxic in its effect to jar or insult, today, the inclusion of all the previously taboo curses and epithets in print, on television, in everyday speech, on buses, trains and in pubs, has become mundane – even boring.

There are those who argue that this is a good thing. An eminent English professor of my acquaintance told me over lunch at The

Garrick Club that 'draining the poison' from previously shocking words is a force for good. His one exception was blasphemy, which can still cause great hurt to those of a religious turn of mind. I'm not sure that he is right about that in our increasingly secular society.

The other phenomenon about the change in 'bad' language in recent years is that its usage has crossed the gender divide. If you have ever listened to a group of 'ladettes' in a pub on a girls' night out, you will have heard language that could strip the enamel off your back teeth.

So, how are we old people supposed to deal with this situation? For sure as heck it's not going to get any better. There will be no return to people coyly covering their mouths with their hand and saying 'pardon my French' when they've uttered the word 'damn'.

I think we would make no attempt to emulate the young and fill the air with 'effing and blinding' but, instead, we might develop a vocabulary of oaths, curses and insults better suited to our mature years and life experience. (My wife has reminded me that this is advice I have so far failed to take myself. Sorry, folks.) I'm particularly drawn to those elaborate curses used by Arabian potentates in the eighteenth century. For example, whereas your young foul-mouth might call somebody 'an effing dickhead' you, on the other hand, could deliver the following magisterial rebuke: 'you are the diseased, illegitimate son of a humpbacked toad and a lame camel' or 'you are the poisonous slime of a serpent's fang' or even 'your mother was the whore of Babylon'.

A bit 'wordy'? Yes, they are, but I can guarantee they will cut through any dinner party conversation with much more effect than any of the old four letter words.

One caveat, however, is that if you accidentally bang your thumb with a hammer while hanging a picture it is unlikely that you will cry out involuntarily: 'Oh, may acid rain from the bowels of Beelzebub flay the flesh from your bones'. Instead, I'm afraid you'll blurt out one of the 'oldies'.

Finally, there is a code of conduct for old people as far as swearing is concerned. The following may be sworn at, cursed and generally abused, but in a jovial, caring way:

- traffic wardens
- other motorists
- accountants

- politicians
- most TV celebrities

You will notice that Inland Revenue Inspectors and Customs Officers are not included. I'm not bloody daft, you know.

Quick Quote:

Perhaps one has to

be very old before

one learns to be

amused rather than

shocked.

Pearl Buck

T

Tachycardia

You may not be aware of your heart beating when suddenly it starts pounding like a trip hammer – 70 beats a minute becomes 120 or 180, even 200 beats in a very short space of time. This might be OK if you've just seen that girl in a bikini drift past your lounger (or, if you're a woman, you've seen a photograph of George Clooney with his shirt unbuttoned). However, if a rapid heartbeat comes on for no apparent reason, you must see your doctor, and as soon as possible. They may diagnose tachycardia and give you a few hints on how you can prevent it from occurring again. If, however, they diagnose ventricular tachycardia, this is an altogether more serious situation. This can be life threatening.

Let's assume all you've experienced is a mild form of rapid heartbeat. If your atria, the chambers in your heart that receive blood and pump it into the ventricles, have got a little out of control (more than 100 beats a minute is a warning sign), my doctor offers the following tips:

1. Slow down. Chill out. Rest.

2. Break the coffee habit. Indeed, avoid stimulants of any kind.

3. Ingest more magnesium (soya beans, nuts and bran).

4. Ingest more potassium (fruit and vegetables).

5. Do a little more exercise.

But, and this is important, even if your sudden increase in heartbeat is mild – go to your doctor anyway. No ifs and no buts. Just go. You know it makes sense.

PS I've listed five tips – here is a sixth, which will reduce rapid heartbeats. Don't watch party political broadcasts on television or listen to John Humphrys hammering some cretinous political oaf into the ground like a tent peg on Radio Four's *Today* programme.

Tattoos

Should old people who have never in their youth enjoyed the subtle pleasure of having a whiskery man in a vest with two teeth missing plunge a needle full of coloured ink into their arms, chest, forehead or buttocks do so now?

I think not. With one exception. For those of you who are suffering more than the usual number of senior moments and are a bit fearful that this heralds the onset of Alzheimer's, I recommend that they have their name and address tattooed on one hand and the phone number of the local hospital on the other. A small butterfly could be added just to complete the picture.

PS An 83-year-old in Manchester is reported to have had a Manchester United logo tattooed on his bottom.

I think death by stoning may be too good for him.

Taxation

We are all familiar with that old cliché that claims there are only two certainties in life – death and taxation. This may be a blunderingly obvious truth, but to old-age pensioners, it has a chilling ring. To many, death itself doesn't herald the end of taxation; inheritance tax, for example, lives on like Dracula rising from his earth-filled tomb to fasten his fangs in the neck of his grieving descendants.

A fortunate few are able to organise their affairs so that long before their demise, they have created trusts that effectively keep the long, clawed fingers of the Inland Revenue away from the money left to their children. Even these arrangements, viewed by HM Treasury as a loophole, are under threat by avaricious tax-gatherers. So what's to do?

If you are selfish, spend the lot before you snuff and leave a big fat zero. Tough on the children, perhaps, but modern young people understand; they even joke about it, coining the phrase SKI, when talking of their parents 'Spending the Kids Inheritance'. Another route is to give it all to your children while you are still alive and kicking. And I mean all of it, cash, shares, house, care, the works. All you have to do then is to not die for seven years. You can do that, can't you?

T

Whatever you choose, do keep lobbying the government of the day to repeal or abolish inheritance tax. It is the most iniquitous tax of all. OK, so they've made a start and pushed the threshold up to £600,000. Why not scrap the wretched thing altogether?

Television

The relationship between retired people and television is a curious one. Unlike the toiling masses, whose viewing is largely confined to the evenings, old people can be exposed to the seductive lure of the goggle box all day long. The influence, therefore, of television on the older viewer is either pernicious, life-enhancing or neutral. It can of course be all of these things in the course of a single day.

Let me declare an interest, before we go any further. As mentioned in an earlier section on the BBC, I worked in the world of commercial television for over thirty years and my views are influenced by the fact that I was on the 'supply' side of television rather than the 'receiving' side. But I was, and still am, a fairly keen television viewer.

To many people, television is trivial, even unimportant. In its early days, some thought it positively baleful. Listen to columnist Peter Simple in *The Sunday Telegraph* on 11 August 1991:

> It is arguable that television is the greatest single evil in the world today. This most superfluous of inventions first became noticeable in England about forty years ago.

> At first it seemed a fascinating toy, a comparatively harmless novelty. What a transformation!! Since then it has developed with the horrible irresistible swiftness of a nightmare into a monstrous all pervading plague. Obedient to the laws which govern our society, it has become an ever proliferation industry employing hundreds of people in the task, by now routine, of purveying ever more of its illusory images making thousands of talentless, often vacuous people rich, famous and powerful merely by being connected with it; perverting and corrupting everything it touches.

> It represents the lowest common denominator of our world; it is the unmistakable voice of the subhuman.

After rereading that, I have come to the conclusion that it's a miracle I'm still alive after spending thirty-three years in the television industry. Of course, this view, written seventeen years ago, is an extreme one. Television can play a very positive role in the lives of old people. Especially those who live alone and whose visits from friends and relatives are few and far between.

At its best, television is a true window on the world, bringing to people sights and sounds that would have seemed miraculous to earlier generations. Any advice I give about television viewing, bearing in mind my background, is likely to sound patronising, so I won't, save for just this: avoid grazing. I know modern producers tend to believe the average viewer has the attention span of a gnat and therefore make programmes that serve up what we call 'bite-size pieces'. But to get the best from your television, be choosy, identify your interests and stick to programmes that genuinely entertain, educate and inform. Always watch the news on at least two channels and if you live alone and are subject to depression, don't watch EastEnders on BBC One or Big Brother on Channel Four. Not only will these programmes destroy your faith in human nature, they will also cause you to lose the will to live.

Telltale Signs of Age

Never mind if well-meaning friends tell you, 'You don't look your age.' They are just being kind. It's up to you to make a judgement about your own ageing process. Here are ten things to watch for:

1. Your ears are hairier than your head

2. You get out of breath playing Ludo

3. Your friends compliment you on your alligator shoes when you are barefoot

4. You can remember when the Dead Sea was just ill

5. You bite into a steak and your teeth stay there

6. When dressing in the morning, you put both legs down one panthole and walk funny all day

7. You no longer think of 30 mile speed signs as just a suggestion

8. If your doctor asks if you have mutual orgasms you say, 'No, I'm with the Prudential'

9. You cut out reports in Which on the quality of toilet paper and paste them in your scrapbook

10. If a nymphomaniac waitress asks you discreetly whether you'd like super-sex, you say 'I'll take the soup'

Quick Quote:

What do you call

a woman who knows

where her husband is

every night? A widow.

Theatre

Even though you may not have been a regular theatregoer in previous years, now you are an old-age pensioner, this could be the time to start. Live theatre can be most entertaining and although I am personally a frequent visitor to my local cinema complex, nothing really compares with seeing actors and actresses in the flesh, strutting their stuff just for you. Check out your local theatre or repertory company – there is likely to be one fairly close to where you live (unless it's a crofter's hut in Scotland or a tent on Dartmoor). Most local theatres give discounts to oldsters and many of them stage plays prior to the West End, so you don't have to pay through the nose to enjoy top-quality performances. Your local paper will keep you up to date with current and forthcoming shows.

I have been a theatregoer for well over a half a century and a well-chosen play or musical can be one of the most rewarding evenings out possible. Some of my most cherished memories are of having seen many of our greatest actors and actresses perform live on stage during the last fifty years. I still recall, with renewed pleasure, Laurence Olivier's performance as Othello at The Old Vic in London in the sixties. And, of course, many, many more, too numerous to mention.

What if you don't fancy an evening out? Or travelling at night? Or missing your early bedtime? Well, how about a matinee? It's a great way to spend an afternoon, cheaper, too, and you can still get home to watch television.

But, be warned. After live theatre, the telly looks boring, drab and faintly unreal.

Trees

Trees are the lungs of the earth and it should be of concern to us all, not just old people, that vast tracts of the rainforest in South America and elsewhere are being destroyed each year. Massive trees are like old people, often gnarled, occasionally bent, but frequently majestic. Old people should love trees and those with large enough gardens should plant a new sapling every time a grandchild is born.

A wealthy friend of mine who is ninety said his father planted a new tree when he was born and now they stand side by side, full of wisdom and fine lines of age.

If you've got a mature tree in your garden or there is one on the street where you live, go and give it a hug – every day – and to hell with what people think.

Truman (President Harry Truman)

Why him? Why an American President? Well, because he is famous for one particular saying and we could all learn from this, so pay attention.

Other great world leaders have left their words of wisdom to posterity ... Winston Churchill, of course, left many my favourite being 'We shall never surrender'. US President Jack Kennedy uttered the famous words 'Ask not what your country can do for you, but what you can do for your country'. Joe Stalin posed the immortal question during the Second World War 'How many divisions does the Pope have?'

Are you still with me? Pretty profound stuff, I think you'll agree. So why Truman? Well, cop a load of this, folks, this is what Harry Truman is famous for having said: 'Never kick a fresh turd in hot weather'. Pretty cute, eh? I only suggest he might have added: especially if you are wearing open-toed sandals.

If you are over sixty-five, start working on your 'final words' for posterity now. If you wait until your last gasp, they are likely to be something like 'a-aaargh!'

Quick Quote:

Die my dear doctor,

that is the last thing I shall do.

Lord Palmerston on his deathbed

U

Umpires (Athletics)

Usually old men wearing blazers, straw hats and flannel trousers. The older the umpire at an athletic event, the longer will be the delay between the command 'get set' and the firing of the starter pistol. This is the reason why there are so many false starts in the 100 metres.

The silly old coot who has called out 'to your marks' and 'get set' has forgotten that he is supposed to fire the bloody pistol, until he is reminded by a semaphore signal from the stands.

If the flag-waving Johnny in the stands is a septuagenarian, too, the race may never ever start. International sprinters have been known to die of malnutrition while waiting for the damn pistol to go off.

Quick Quote:

Whenever I feel the

urge to exercise, I lay

down until the feeling

wears off.

Oscar Wilde

Umpires (Cricket)

Only old people should be cricket umpires and I mean very old people, who can't count up to six without a pocket of pebbles to help them. They should look quite relaxed at the wicket, even though they are wearing five players' discarded pullovers round their shoulders. They should also be short-sighted, obstinate, overweight and jowly and have a depth of ignorance about the rules of cricket, only to be plumbed perhaps by the fruit fly.

Undergarments

There is, it must be confessed, not a great deal of media interest in what old people wear next to their skin. Even hardened readers of the *Sun* or the *News of the World* would blanch at the prospect of a double-page spread in colour with photographs of geriatric knicker fashions. But old people do wear undergarments of a staggering variety. I myself, at age seventy-four, still possess a collection that would alarm Mr Tom Jones, the international warbler, who has had such a superabundant selection of French knickers, thongs, jockstraps and bloomers thrown at him on stage while performing that he is acknowledged as being one of the world's experts on the subject of underclothing. The only items I abhor in this vast range are the cream-coloured Y-fronts, perhaps the world's most unsexy piece of clothing ever invented.

However, whether your choice is jockey shorts, baggy pants or, in the case of ladies, frilly bloomers, change them every two days. This is a must. No ifs. No buts. You see, my research among many thousands of 30-year-olds has revealed with stunning clarity that they believe, with a powerful conviction no logic or arguments can gainsay, that old people never change their underwear.

So, to counteract this malign slur on us oldies – change your underpants or knickers every two days. Without fail. OK, three days, at the most. And the full wash if you don't mind, none of your hand rinsing in a plastic bowl. That will not do, thank you very much. And changing them from back to front instead of washing won't do, either. Or suffer the indignity of a lingering death on some hospital slab while the giggling surgeon and his tittering assistants slice away your disgusting, six-month-old Y-fronts with a blowtorch before they can perform that life-saving intervention that in any case has come too late.

Quick Quote:

If you can eat a

boiled egg at ninety

in England, they

think you deserve a Nobel Prize.

Alan Bennett

The Upper Reaches of the Nile

A place old people should visit. In this tropical, forested paradise lives a tribe called The Dinkas. They are a splendid people, very tall and slim, and it is not uncommon for some of them to live until they are over 100 years old. No pot bellies or sagging boobs here among the jolly old Dinkas. Diet is believed to be a major factor both in their longevity and in their slimness. Root vegetables and small creepy-crawlies seem to be the favourite choice.

However, when you get home to your semi in Pinner, Penge or Plymouth, it's no good emulating the Dinkas by smearing your naked body with ash, swallowing a ladybird and herding long-horned cattle through the garden with a pointed stick, it's too late. You should have visited when you were eighteen or less.

Maybe, on reflection, you shouldn't visit the Upper Reaches of The Nile, after all. Stick to Florida, where everybody will be older, fatter and uglier than you. This will make you feel good and you won't have to crunch on a beetle, either.

Quick Quote:

Anyone can get old.

All you have to do

is live long enough.

Groucho Marx

V

Varicose Veins

I'm sorry about all these nasty subjects that keep cropping up in what I hope is a fairly cheeky book, but let's face it, varicose veins do happen to old folk quite a lot. Not exclusively, of course, but frequently enough to be a real problem for people in retirement.

First of all, cosmetically, they are ugly. Like bits of knotted string lurking just below the skin's surface. Worse, of course, for women, who wear skirts or dresses. Men are lucky enough to hide them behind trousers and socks. So what exactly are they?

Varicose veins are veins that have become weakened and are no longer capable of performing their vital function of returning blood to the heart, rather like a train that runs out of steam and can't make the return journey.

The condition is not life threatening, but can lead to aching limbs and general listlessness. Occasionally, the varicose vein sufferer will suffer from either clotting or rupture. This is rare, but serious. If it happens to you, off to the doctor at once. But for most of you with those knotty protuberances in the calf and ankle area, here are a few tips:

1. Get gravity on your side. Get your feet up. Regularly.

2. Wear tight socks or a support hose.

3. Try tilting your bed, so when you sleep your feet are a little higher than your head. Be careful though, lifting can put your back out (see 'B' for Backache).

4. Stay away from excessively tight-fitting clothes. Apart from the fact that old people in skintight Lycra look positively repulsive, tight clothes act like a tourniquet, especially girdles or belts, as they will keep your blood pooled in your legs. A ghastly prospect, is it not? Just visualise some old duffer tottering about with a

white face drained of all colour and legs like a moonscape, all lumps and ridges and bright purple, too. So loose clothes, please, but not so loose that your pants fall down. Just be sensible. Do you hear that, Granny? Yes, I know you'll be sensible, but what about him?

5. Keep moving. Exercise will help that sluggish blood to circulate.

6. If you are still worried about your varicose veins, even though you've followed the above advice, do go and see your GP.

> **Quick Quote:**
>
> My husband suffers
>
> from tired blood.
>
> When he gets up in
>
> the morning, his
>
> blood stays in bed
>
> for another half hour.
>
> Phyllis Diller (American Comedienne)

Venice

Old people should visit Venice not just because it is the most achingly beautiful city in the world, but because of its striking similarity with the state of retirement itself.

Without stretching the analogy to breaking point, just consider how, for example, the City of Venice compares with an elderly narcissistic lady in a comfortable nursing home. Her previous life over, consumed by the passage of time, but flashes of earlier brilliance remain. In spite of the fissures and blemishes on her face, her eyes, windows to the soul, still sparkle and shine.

The City of Venice is in a state of voluptuous retirement. Its old life and its purpose are long gone, but hints of earlier grandeur are everywhere. For more than a thousand years, Venice was unique among the nations of the world, hanging like a glittering jewel between Rome and Byzantium, encircled by the vastness of the Adriatic and being both Asian and European, half Christian, half Muslim.

V

I have been in love with Venice for more than thirty years now and I try to visit at least once every twelve months. Since retiring, the effect this fabulous, man-made miracle has had on me is quite remarkable. It is as if my senses have been sharpened to better appreciate its sights, smells and sounds.

If you haven't been yet, go, and go soon, for Serenissima is old, retired and dying. She will, however, outlive you and your grandchildren, in spite of all the talk of sinking and disappearing under the eccentric tides of the Adriatic. So go and walk the warren of streets and listen to the slap of water against the gleaming, sleek black sides of the gondolas. Touch with your fingers the peeling stucco of the ancient palaces, still breathtakingly beautiful, with their soaring Gothic windows and their geranium-draped stone balconies. Stand in St Marks Square at dawn's first light, while the old lady still sleeps, and hear your own heartbeat quicken as you gaze at the lunatic extravagance of the great Basilica, with its domes and minarets and crumbling stonework.

Later, take coffee at Florian's in the square and perhaps enjoy a trip along the canals in a gondola. It is not necessary to go into a museum in Venice, or even an art gallery, although they are numerous, as the city itself is a museum and every building, every piazza, every serpentine bridge, every church is a work of art. And Venetians are traditionally long-lived, so old people feel at home in the city. Giovanni Bellini died at eighty-six, Titian at eighty-eight and Sansovino at ninety-one.

Avoid the high tourist season. In the summer months, Venice resembles downtown Tokyo crammed with Japanese tourists, whose incessant clicking of cameras resembles a plague of cicadas noisily rubbing their back legs together.

Go beyond the great square of St Marks and get deliciously lost in its labyrinthine backstreets. Surprises and architectural delights await you at almost every turn.

So go. Please. And go soon. Venice is like a gorgeously faded courtesan, she welcomes any number of discerning new lovers and she never disappoints.

Last, and perhaps most important of all, don't stay more than three days and nights. You can absorb so much of her splendour in this short time and leave with your hunger still intact, ready for the next visit, and the next, and the next.

Quick Quote:

The most triumphant

city I have ever set

eyes on. A place of

silks and emeralds and

marbles and brocades

and velvets and lace,

of stupendous palaces

and limpid canals and

glittering barges and

great galleon vessels.

> Anon (Although I like to think this was said by Marco
> Polo, himself a Venetian)

Verruca

Oh alright, I know what a verruca is now. Now I've read its definition in *Cassell's English Dictionary*, it is a wart-like elevation, a sort of scaly lump old people find on the soles of their feet. With a slight change of spelling, for example, exchanging the 'c' for a 'g', it becomes something thrillingly exotic – a disease characterised by ulcerous lumps that are endemic in Peru!

So there we are then. The next time you put your socks on, hold a mirror against the soles of your feet and see if you've got a touch of the Peruvian nasties. Mind you, if your last six holidays were in Frinton, I doubt if you've actually succumbed to the dreaded disease of the Andes mountain chain. Never mind. Life can be quite cruel.

But I digress. Let's get back to verruca. Before I checked it out in my old, dog-eared Cassell's, I was convinced, and I mean convinced, dear reader, that Verruca was the name of a tall, willowy ash-blonde actress, with thighs like columns of marble and lips so full and rounded she could suck an egg out of a chicken.

Did I imagine this? Was I fantasising? (Who gives a shit anyway?) I've blown it. You now know what a 'real' verruca is and much good will it do you. Sorry about that. Do read on.

Vertigo

Old people staggering about and falling down doesn't always mean they've been at the sweet sherry or enjoying one of their grandchildren's funny cigarettes. It may mean they are suffering from orthostatic vertigo, which is usually caused by a sudden drop in blood pressure.

The most common cause of mild vertigo is hypotension; you stand up suddenly and whoa, the head spins and you feel dizzy. Some blood pressure pills (like mine) can contribute to this condition, especially if they are a diuretic. A diuretic, as every schoolboy knows, makes you wee copiously. It's bad luck if you leap up from a nap, bursting for a leak, go all dizzy, fall over and wet your pants. Honestly, Grandad, get a grip of yourself. Seriously though, mild dizziness is nothing to worry about. Falling down is.

The other common causes of dizziness are:

a. Viral Infection known as Labyrinthitis, which sounds very sinister, but is actually inflammation of the fluid-filled ear canals.

b. Low blood sugar – sometimes occurs if you miss a meal.

c. Menopause, except for blokes. Lucky swine.

d. Migraine sensory disturbance, which can be triggered by chocolate, cheese or red wine.

e. Anaemia. Low red blood count (that's you, paleface).

If dizziness persists, it's round to the doctor if you please.

Vick

This is a fine product designed to ease the breathing and relieve cold symptoms, such as a sore throat. Anybody over sixty-five should have an industrial-sized vat of the stuff in the house at all times.

Although not recommended by the makers, I have found two slices of brown bread lightly spread with Vick a great comfort during those cold snaps in November. I should confess here that I was not wearing my glasses at the moment of spreading and had assumed the pungent jelly I was using was greengage jam.

PS I have also found Vick a great help in easing stiff locks, although the results are not permanent. OK, OK, this particular experiment was after three quarters of a bottle of claret and a tiny snifter of brandy.

W

Walking Sticks

Even if you feel you don't actually need one yet, go out and purchase one today. A fine walking stick gives an old person an air of gravitas and authority, especially if it has been carefully chosen. Avoid those hideous fake jobs, fashioned from some revolting man-made fibre or fancy plastic. Pick one that has been hewn from an ancient English tree and has been polished and shaped by craftsmen.

I have a collection of walking sticks, gathered over the years from various parts of the world, but my favourite is a splendid fellow made from English ash. Swinging down your high street with a fine walking stick adds a jaunty spring to your step and sends out a subtle message to all those whose paths cross yours. 'Stand aside and let a gentleman pass through'. (For ladies, a large brimmed hat worn with an air of reckless insouciance serves much the same purpose.)

Warts

I've had them. Maybe you have, too. My mum knew how to get rid of them when I was a young lad. Take a knob of butter, slap it on the warty protrusion and let it melt slowly over a hot fire, while muttering a gypsy curse. Difficult, I will admit, if you have a wart on your nose. Did it work? I've no idea; it's too long ago to remember.

A learned doctor in Florida, USA, claims that vitamin E is the thing for warts. Many people, the medico claims, report that applying a cream of 28,000 IUs of vitamin E to a wart once or twice a day helps to get rid of them. Plus, taking 400 IUs of vitamin E orally each day. Well, if you can believe that guff, you can believe anything – 28,000! That's a lot of IUs (and what in heaven's name is an IU?).

So, if you are a warthog sort of person, either put up with the condition and proudly show off your warts at social gatherings or try my mum's method. All you need for this is an open fire and a wart that is not in an inaccessible position. Oh, yes, and a knob of butter;

155

I favour Anchor myself. Unless, of course, you can actually count to 28,000 IUs.

PS Any good chemists do a 'freezing' liquid for warts which really works. It's called Wartnell, but do follow the instructions carefully.

PPS The late Nikita Khrushchev of the Soviet Union once described America as 'A wart on the buttock of humanity'.

Weight

Being overweight is now becoming something of an epidemic and that includes old people, too. The most starkly simple solution to being overweight is to eat less!

However, for the purists among you, here is a table detailing the calories used up per hour for various kinds of daily activities old people might indulge in. Make of it what you will:

Activity	Calories per hour
Bowling	264
Gardening (light)	220
Golf	300
Mowing the lawn	462
Eating whilst seated	84
Sleeping	60
Pole vaulting in an astronaut's padded suit and lead-lined moon boot	2,793 and a half

Wellington (the Boot and the Duke)

There is not a great deal I wish to say about the wellington boot. Most of us have owned a pair and jolly useful they are, too, for pottering about in the garden.

What I do wish to say about The Duke of Wellington could take at least a book and a half, so I'll be brief. He was, I submit, the greatest Englishman who ever lived, even though he was part Irish. In my view, a splendid combination.

He was only forty-five when he defeated Napoleon at The Battle of Waterloo, but then went on to become Prime Minister twice and he was, in his day, as popular and as feted as any modern pop star or Hollywood superstar.

His funeral drew a crowd of over a million, lining the streets of London as his cortège passed by. His defeat of the French, both at Waterloo and in the earlier Peninsular War, was as significant to the way we live now as was the struggle against Hitler's Nazi Germany.

He might be a shade too patrician for modern tastes; he was certainly elitist, but he embodied all the characteristics that are so often lacking in today's political leaders. And he lived to the age of eighty-three, quite a feat in 1852.

This was also the year in which my own grandfather was born, himself a career soldier, to whom I salute the memory of the great Duke every year with a glass of champagne on the anniversary of his death, 14 September. And so should you, even with a glass of Wincarnis.

Wife-swapping

Or even husband-swapping, it matters not what gender is on offer, there is a golden rule about this nefarious practice. If you are one of those rare types who goes to suburban parties where such activities take place and some jerk offers to swap his wife with you, don't be offended, but don't offer your own in exchange. Oh no, that would be silly. Say you would be glad to take his missus in return for that old studio couch or black-and-white TV set you've had in the attic for twenty years. He might just accept and bingo, you've got yourself a free home-help to alleviate your own dear spouse's domestic burdens.

I've often thought about writing to the American film star Michael Douglas and offering him a three-piece suite in return for Catherine Zeta-Jones.

Quick Quote:

A titled lady was

once asked whether

she had ever

contemplated divorcing

her errant husband.

'Divorce? Never,' was

her succinct reply,

'but murder, frequently.'

Anon

Wrinkles (see also 'D' for dry skin)

You're reading this book, chances are you've got wrinkles. Maybe a few, just around the eyes, but you've got 'em. Perhaps you have lots of wrinkles, great crevices and dried up river beds of wrinkles that criss-cross your face and neck. Well, should you contemplate plastic surgery, or a facelift, or a head transplant?

That, dear reader, is a matter of personal choice. I happen to think that old folk who do have one of the various treatments on offer today, risk looking horribly unnatural. We've all seen those ageing film stars, usually American, who have had a facelift or Botox injections and they look, to me at least, quite unreal.

The old skin has been tightened and now has a texture of corpse-like blandness. However, I'm sure a modest treatment, if you can afford it, can be helpful to one's self esteem. But if you are worried about your wrinkles and the idea of the surgeon's knife or the plastic implant doesn't appeal, try this:

> Egg whites. Try an egg-white face mask to make your skin
> smoother. Egg white is made of water and albumin proteins
> that can nourish the skin, because as the water evaporates,
> the proteins dry on. When you wash off the hardened
> mask, it takes away dead cells, making the skin smoother
> and healthier looking.

It won't cure wrinkles and it's not a panacea, but it can have an alleviating effect and half a dozen eggs are a lot cheaper than flying to Los Angeles to have your head peeled by a mad Chinese-American, who also specialises in cosmetically dressing corpses for bereaved relatives before interment.

PS (This PS is for those of you who don't fancy an eggy face.) Our TV screens are bulging with advertisements offering creams and lotions that will 'reduce the appearance' of wrinkles. They are expensively packaged, expensively priced and they contain new chemicals with unpronounceable names.

So all they do is 'reduce the appearance' of wrinkles. Big deal. It would be cheaper to slap on a bit of stage make-up that would do the trick at a fraction of the price. Because you're worth it!

Writing

Yes, joined-up writing. Not texting, emailing or producing round-robin letters on the computer, but one-to-one handwritten communications on proper notepaper and placed in envelopes on which the address is also handwritten and a stamp affixed before posting in a red pillar box.

I'm sure most of you still do, even though your letters have fallen off in recent years and have been replaced by postcards. But writing letters to friends and family is the duty of old people. If we don't keep it up, the whole skill of handwriting will disappear. I will confess that my own joined-up handwriting is pretty poor, but I write in block capitals and have done for years.

So avoid the horror of texting, in spite of all that pressure from your grandchildren. Write to them, in your very best handwriting. Your letters could become collectors' pieces in about fifty-years time – if not before.

> **Quick Quote:**
>
> I don't believe in
>
> an afterlife although
>
> I am bringing a
>
> change of underwear.
>
> Woody Allen

X

X-rays

Always ask the nurse for copies of any X-rays you are required to endure. I think some new Brussels law makes it impossible for the hospital to refuse you. You can always crop them and stick them in the family photo album alongside those holiday snaps. Think of the hours of pleasure you will get on those long winter evenings, thumbing through black-and-white images of your lower intestine, accompanied by a glass of Madeira. I can think of nothing better to do on a wet Friday in December. It certainly beats watching EastEnders, although I have found that after five or six glasses of Madeira, I can never quite determine whether I'm watching my own insides or a knees-up in the Queen Vic.

And have you noticed how your dentist runs out of the room before he X-rays your teeth? OK, I know it's a safety measure, as they mustn't overexpose themselves to radiation, but must they run? Anyone would think they were about to detonate a high explosive. I always insist my dentist walks casually from the room. It is so much more calming.

Y

Yanks

OK, I should have put this piece under 'A' for Americans, but I didn't want to upset our transatlantic cousins so early in this little book. So Yanks it is.

I believe it was George Bernard Shaw who said the English and the Americans were 'separated by a common language'. This is no less true today than when GBS uttered it (unless it was Dorothy Parker).

Today, many Americanisms have drifted into our everyday speech, along with many habits that affect the way we live, consume, play and work. Let me state here and now that many of these influences have been benign or even dynamic. The great American trait of enthusiasm has been a tonic to our traditionally laid-back way of life. However, there are some things that would have been better left on the other side of the Atlantic. I need cite only a few:

- The baseball cap
- McDonald's
- The Hawaiian shirt
- Sylvester Stallone
- The phrase 'mudderfucka' (don't ask)

Music and cinema were two huge influences on my life as a youngster in London. In the late forties and fifties, 'pop' music was almost exclusively American and very good a lot of it was, too. Sinatra, Crosby, Louis Armstrong, Frankie Laine, swing jazz and big band music, too, with many movie music themes becoming classics in their own right.

It was only in the early sixties that British popular music took over, when the Beatles and others conquered the world by storm. But the American influence remained and reached well beyond the world of music. I can remember the thrill of walking into a black-and-white milk bar and ordering a strawberry milkshake. Luxury beyond compare to a 12-year-old London lad, whose preferred soft drink was either lemonade

163

or Tizer. You remember Tizer, don't you? A sort of orange-coloured fizz that made you burp through your nose.

At the time of writing, America remains the most powerful nation on earth and, more importantly, our most vital ally. Whatever criticisms we make of America, and I am one who takes a shot at some of their most ludicrous absurdities, we must never forget that without America's strong arm we, the British, would be a good deal less safe and free than we are today. Occasionally irritating, sometimes brash, but when it comes to the crunch, as solid as a rock.

In terms of consumer innovation and comfort, the Americans lead the world, but by the time my grandchildren are grandparents themselves, indeed long before then, Uncle Sam will have been overtaken as the primary superpower by China. After China? Who knows. Maybe oil-rich Russia and rapidly modernising India.

Splendid though these countries are in their own way, we British must never try to replace America as our number one ally and partner; our friendship is long and deep and our mutual trust must never be compromised. We oldies must keep that flame of comradeship burning and pass the torch on to our children in the English-speaking world.

Yawning

As *Cassell's English Dictionary* reminds us, a yawn is 'to gape' or 'to have the mouth open involuntarily through drowsiness, boredom or bewilderment'.

Old people yawn a lot. So do almost any age group, when they are drowsy, bored or bewildered. No, Grandad, it's not the same as being 'bewitched, bothered and bewildered', that was a fifties pop song. But the yawn, for we oldies, is particularly fraught with dangers. It may be a natural thing to do when we are drowsy, oh alright, I won't go through it all again but, unlike the sneeze (see 'S' for Sneezing), you should try to control a yawn.

So if to let a sneeze rip is OK, why not a yawn? Well, because if you open your mouth too widely, you can be in danger of dislocating your jaw. Cases of jaws locking in mid yawn may be rare, but when they do occur, they tend to be among the over sixty-fives. In extreme cases, people with locked jaws can feel as if they are choking, because of the build up of saliva in their mouths.

Doctors advise old people who are frozen in mid yawn to bend forwards or lie on their sides in the recovery position, to let gravity ease the pressure. To re-set a locked jaw, dentists push the lower jaw downwards and back, by pushing on the lower back teeth. That's all very well, I hear you cry, but what about if you haven't got any back teeth left? What to do then? Frankly, I've no idea. Unless you just push on the gums.

On a lighter note, I have always enjoyed these press photographs of dignitaries at some formal function caught yawning at the wrong moment. Ex-prime minister's wife Cherie Blair comes to mind. I also remember the late Frank Muir saying that the only thing he learnt from sitting on some deeply boring BBC committee was how to yawn with the mouth shut.

Don't try it though. Just cover the yawn with your hand or the programme of one of Harold Pinter's stage plays. And don't open too wide!

Yodelling

I have only ever seen fat, old people yodelling and they were in leather shorts and little hats with shaving brushes stuck in the brim. Oh yes, and they were foreign.

If it ever catches on in this country, it will probably be in Bournemouth and I think the authorities should clamp down on it with great severity. This great nation of ours, raised on roast beef, rain, unpunctual trains and the Last Night of the Proms at the Albert Hall, do not wish to be corrupted by any sort of Teutonic tonsil wobbling.

OK, so we drive BMWs and Mercedes and we have been known to nibble the occasional black sausage (not to mention a Black Forest gateau). But yodelling. Never. Raise a petition among the old people living in your nearest retirement home and stop the tide of yodelling from ever swamping our shores.

PS Imagine, if you can, some Euro law from Brussels making it compulsory for various traditional activities from different European countries to be merged. You could get yodelling while performing the morris dancing routine in a kilt and wooden clogs, accompanied, of course, by a German oompah band.

Z

Z-z-z-z-z (Snoring)

The sound old people make when they sleep, unless the z-z-z-z-z is punctuated by a series of snores that could easily be mistaken for a circus strongman tearing in half a roll of calico. If you or your partner snores, try ramming a knob of butter up each nostril before you go to bed. Will this top the snoring? Not necessarily, but it sure as hell will prevent you from falling asleep and thus your partner and you can enjoy a snore free night.

Seriously though, how do you know if you are a heavy or moderate snorer? If your wife or your husband moves out of the bedroom, you snore at a moderate level. If your neighbours move then you're a heavy snorer.

An actual snore is caused by the tissue in the upper airway in the back of the throat becoming relaxed, when it vibrates. The effect is not dissimilar to a wind instrument. Sadly, most people's snores don't sound remotely like an oboe, a flute or a saxophone. More's the pity.

The only real tips my doctor has given me about snoring are:

1. Avoid large pillows. They put a kink in your neck, which accentuates snoring.

2. Avoid alcohol prior to retiring.

3. Buy your partner earmuffs.

Finally, the world's loudest snore was recorded by a 250 lb British man, Mr Melvin Switzer. According to the *Guinness Book of Records*, Melvin registered 88 decibels, the same intensity as a motorcycle being revved at full throttle.

Sweet dreams.

Zen And The Art Of Gentle Retirement

Zen Buddhism is a Japanese school of twelfth-century Chinese origin that teaches contemplation of a person's essential nature to the total exclusion of everything else. Practitioners insist that this is the only way of achieving pure enlightenment. Have you got that?

Good, because I don't want you to confuse Zen with Zoroastrianism, the Dualistic religion founded by the Persian Prophet Zoroaster in the seventh century BC, which laid out the confused scribbling, sorry, the sacred writings of the Zend-Avesta.

As every schoolboy and old-age pensioner knows, the sacred writings of the Zend-Avesta are based on the concept of a continuous struggle between Ahura Mazda, the God of wisdom, light and all nice goodies and his hated arch enemy Ahriman, the spirit of evil, darkness, pimples and constipation. Oh, alright, this is getting silly and before you ask, Ahura Mazda did not invent a small Japanese motor car.

However, contemplation and peaceful inner thoughts are things that we old people should practise from time to time. Away from the hustle and bustle of everyday life, work and other people, setting aside half an hour a day just to sit, or preferably lie down, and think alone is a very therapeutic exercise, indeed. And, Grandad, this is not the same as zonking out on the sofa after two pints of Wincarnis and half a gallon of Guinness.

Old people who live alone are probably doing this far more than for half an hour a day and for them, my advice is quite different. Spending all day just with your own thoughts is a step too far, so try, if you can, to get out a little more, phone a friend or turn on the radio. I make this suggestion seriously, because loneliness is not a thing to be treated with levity.

For those of us who are still leading busy lives even in retirement, a slice of your day spent in simple contemplation is very rewarding. So do give it a go. Start tomorrow.

Quick Quote:

This book should

not be tossed aside

lightly. It should

be hurled with great force.

Dorothy Parker

Epilogue

Why 'Zen' and 'The Art of Gentle Retirement'? Well, it seemed a good idea at the time I started this book. The 'Zen' bit was, I admit, designed to catch your attention and if you've read this far, it clearly worked.

I mean, *Monty Phython's Flying Circus* was a hugely successful TV series, which had absolutely nothing to do with snakes, circuses or flying. I had originally thought of giving this book a much more outrageous, eye-catching title like: Underwater Masturbation for the Deaf, but my wife threatened to strangle me if I did. So I didn't.

I'm off for my nap now – thanks for reading.

Harry Turner